FOR THE SAKE *of*

My Children

To Pastor Ron, Karen
Keep on doing the work
of the Father!!
Y Willis
2019

YVONNE WHITE

ISBN 978-1-64492-726-7 (paperback)
ISBN 978-1-64492-727-4 (digital)

Christian Faith Publishing, Inc.
832 Park Avenue
Meadville, PA 16335
www.christianfaithpublishing.com

Printed in the United States of America

ACKNOWLEDGEMENTS

To my children Mark, Sarah, Jhaun-Paul, Ronneka, and R.J., for loving me unconditionally, and in loving memory of my daughter, Jodi, who was taken from us too soon.

To my parents Delores and Leebert; thank you for the gift of life. To my brothers and sisters, Althea, Angella, Loveaet, Denise (Sweets), Kelisha, 'Dimple, Yane, Yanna, Mark, Henry, Leon, Kirk and 'Sackie'. Thank you all for being there for me along the many twists and turns in my life.

Thanks also to Pastor Ron Stein, Kim and my church family, Carolyn, and my fabulous co-workers at the hospital. Support comes in so many ways, and the well-timed smile or hug always means so very much.

Additionally, I need to send a special thank you to those who kept my family unit functioning. Aunt Dell, Jasine, Mr. and Mrs. White, and Mr. and Mrs. Hall, I am forever in your debt.

Lastly, I wish to mention a few of my close friends, Karl, Janice and Vickie, who were a part of my support system along this journey. And a special thank you to Wendy, not only for her moral support, but also for bringing my newest friend and closet copy editor into my life. Amy's eye for detail allowed me to remain focused on the big picture, while ensuring the intended meaning of my message came through in my written words.

PREFACE

This book was inspired by an actual event that happened to me at the Black River Courthouse, in Jamaica; July of 2000. I was made redundant from my job sometime in February of that same year, and was experiencing a great deal of stress. As a single parent, I had the responsibility of caring for my children, while their father refused to provide maintenance for them. My only option was to take him to court in order to receive the financial support he was obligated to provide for our children.

During the court appearance, the children's father told the judge he was not employed, which was a lie. I, in return, told the judge that currently I was out of a job also. The judge then turned to me asking, "Don't you hear the man say him not working?" "Your honor, how am I gonna manage to take care of the children on my own?" I asked. The judge's response was "yu shouda know sey yu nah wok before yu go breed, if yu can't manage dem sen dem go poor house." I had been betrayed by a Judge; someone you go to when you are looking for justice.

Not able to provide the basic needs for my children, I had to send them to stay with three different relatives. My world was falling apart, and I was unable to eat or sleep. Ninety percent of these poems were written during those trying times in my life.

There are many forms of physical and psychological abuse that imprint deeply in ones soul. For me as a mother not being able to protect and provide for my children robbed me of the joys of motherhood, and brought back painful childhood memories of not having my mother to love and protect me from things that are too painful to

talk about. She migrated to another country before I was three years old and never took the time to help meet my basic needs.

Now, my only desire is to right the wrong that was done to me, by providing for my children the best way I can. That is why I stay in Iowa and put up with the brutal winters that Iowa is known for, like fifty below and snow covering the front door.

Contents

For The Sake Of My Children

For the sake of my children I am carrying this load,
I have no one to lean on so I stand alone.
My load is heavy and I am light, for the sake of my children,
I will not lie, sometimes I feel like I would die.

Deep in my heart I hear a still, small voice,
Victory is near, don't you quit.
There will be heartaches, headaches, and backaches,
At times even the earth will shake.

If you use your faith it will be a piece of cake,
You will be able to face whatever comes your way.
My wage is low and the bills are high.
At night I lay awake and cry, Dear God, when will this end?

Show me how to make ends meet.
I am standing at the crossroads in my life,
For the sake of my children, I will not run and hide.
With humble pride, I will ride the tide,
For their sake I will go the last mile.

I may be poor, I know I will grow old, but before I do, for the
Sake of my children, I will close the door that leads to poverty.
This I will do to prove to the world that even
Though I stand alone, I am never alone.

My faith and I walk hand in hand,
And even when I am dead and gone
And they commit my body to the land of the dead,
I will be remembered not for the bumps I wear on my face
Caused from stress of caring for my children all on my own.

I am doing my best; I will not bow to the powers
That seem to be telling me to send my children to the poorhouse.

The drums of time are beating faster than you know,
I hope you know my tears will never fall in vain.
I will bear the pain, for in a little while the rain will stop.
I too will see the sun again, it will shine through the eyes of my
Children, for the sake of my children I know it will.

LOVING YOU

I will love you till the day I die,
Please don't ask me why.
I will love you till the world stops spinning,
Loving you is more than life to me

You are the air I breathe,
Without you there would be no me.
I will love you even when you stop loving me,
You are the food I eat to keep my heart pumping.

When I am with you I want to skip and sing,
Sing of all the joys you bring into my life,
Please don't ask me why.

I will love you in the winter and even in the summer,
Together we will live in love and harmony,
And even if you have no money,
You will still be my honey.

I will keep on loving you even when you stop loving me
I will love you until my dying days.

SOME PEOPLE

Some people start at the end,
Some in the middle,

Some are trying to understand the riddle
Are you playing with a fiddle while others sit and giggle?

Some people share their pain,
I feel it is a shame to dwell on pain.
Then again, what do I know about feeling pain.

If you start at the end,
You must still find the beginning.
Maybe you will learn how to win,
If you allow yourself to fall in love again.

Some people will still see the sun long after it is gone.
Some people will find a new love at the end of the sunset.

SLEEPLESS NIGHT

Last night my eyes refused to sleep,
I lay awake all night it seems
Trying to sweep the cobwebs from my mind,

Now I feel like a swine
Trying to unwind with my head
Swinging from side to side.

Yesterday I waited but only in vain,
Now it feels like the blood stopped
Running through my vein,
You are gone on the train

Now I am feeling so frail,
The pain is more than I can bear.
The pain is still in my spine,
I turn on my side like a young swine,
I roll in my misery, still something was missing

I hissed through my teeth and drew the sheet,
But I just could not sleep.
I was waiting for my mystery man who is in great demand.

He was somewhere else having sweet dreams while I screamed
Just to have him in my dream,
How will I dream when my eyes refuse to sleep?

What Do You Want To Be

What do you want to be?
Better to be a little you
Than a lot of someone else living in you.

Unity is strength; find your inner strength.
Live your life while you have time

Climb the ladder of success.
Don't allow yourself to fall off the wall of time.
Take your time; dig deep into the well of understanding,
Make it your undertaking,
Know who you are and live out your dreams.

Never allow yourself to float down the stream of life.
If you do, your brain will be bloated with the pain
Of not achieving anything.

Embrace life; don't let it embrace you,
Or else you will become overwhelmed with life's ups and
downs. Take a break if you must, but don't sit back and rust.

Before too long, you will not be able to hear them say,
"Dust to dust,"
Who do you want to be;
A pile of dust or a mountain of success?
Live your life while you have time.

MOMENTS

If things get worse, it will be a curse.
I don't know the source, all I know it is very coarse.

I have never been the one to boast
I need to find the source of all my pain.
I wish with all my heart that the rain would fall on my head,
And wash away all my fears.

My tears are all I have got
The world has left me to rot.
Sometimes I forget what loving is all about.
Life is a roundabout. I am in a boat
Trying to float on the sea of dryness.

My heart is sad; my head is empty, to the world
It seems that I have plenty, sometimes I wish I were twenty,
Maybe I would not feel so empty

Moments of sadness leave me with dryness
If I were a princess,
I would have all the access to the things I need
To make me happy, for now all I have is stress
If things get any worse, it will be a curse.

MOTHERS

If mothers learn to teach their sons
How to be men
Wives will be able to be a wife to her husband
Instead of trying to be his mother

Teach your sons how to turn youthful lust
Into motivation to work overtime to build
Up a nest egg for his family-to-be

A fool and his money shall soon depart
But a husband who caters to the needs of his wife
Will be king to his tribe

Let's teach our sons money management
Money should be your servant
Take control of your money

Never let money rule you
Buying roses for your wife is good
But treating her like a delicate rose
Is more important than buying her roses

Build your house with bricks of understanding
Furnish it with love and respect

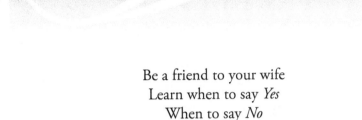

Be a friend to your wife
Learn when to say *Yes*
When to say *No*
Most importantly, learn when not to speak

Son, you cannot buy love
Never try to buy a woman's affection
Because as soon as your money runs out
She will find a new buyer

Stupidity is for fools, my son,
Please, I am begging you
Don't put your heart in the middle of the highway
And not expect it to get run over

I Am Not Trying

I am not trying to fit in
Not trying to be what I am not
Who I am is who I am

I get blamed for living up to what I believe in
I refuse to just live for the moment

People call me names
Still I refuse to play in their games
I am not a woman who is afraid of being herself

I live by my own set of rules
What are these rules, you may ask?

I refused to use people in the name of progress
I try to do as the Good Book says

Do unto others what you want them to do to you
To some I am a nobody
Just because I refuse to listen to everybody
I want to be my own hero

MAMA, PLEASE FORGIVE ME

Mama, I know that I never took the time to listen to you.
I used to tell myself that all you do is talk and talk.

Mama, I took you for granted
Mama, if only I had listened to you instead of my friends

Mama, my freedom would still be mine
Mama, I would not be doing time

Mama, I wish that I could turn back the hands of time
Mama, I would do what you tell me to do
I would clean my room and take out the trash
I would not skip class

Mama, when I was getting drunk and high
My friends were all I needed, or so it seemed

Mama, if I could turn back the hands of time
I would not be doing time
Mama, if only I had listened to you
Mama, please forgive me!

MYRTLE

Who was Myrtle?
Depends on who is asking

To some she was a mother
To some she was a grandmother

To some she was a great-grandmother
To some she was a great-great-grand mother like no other

She was a wife
She was a friend
She was a sister
She was a good neighbor

With nothing in her hand she took care of thirteen children.
She was labeled the community guinea pig.

Ever heard about the lady who lived in a shoe
Who had so many children she did not know what to do

That was not Myrtle
Myrtle was a mover, she was a shaper, she was a warrior
She waged war with poverty; she looked it in the eye and told
Poverty that she will not bow down and serve him

How did she do it?
By teaching her children the value of hard work
Everyone had something to do, no free ride
To be poor is not a crime,
To stay poor because you are too lazy

To work that is a crime,
Myrtle did not wear name-brand clothes
Her kids did not wear brand new clothes

If truth should be told
Sometimes they had to share the same clothes
If you don't believe me, ask my dad
He will tell you that he and his brothers took turns going to school.

'Who's' House

Whose house will the children gather?
Who will tell the stories of the past?
Who will cook the food and spread the table
For the next generation

Give the children roots; make sure you find a way to teach them
The real meaning of family
How can one learn without a teacher?
How can one teach if we burn down the classroom?
We burn the Book of Knowledge, who needs the Golden Rules?

We don't trust in God anymore, we kill our unborn babies
In the name of self-development we take life for granted.
We take guns to school and shoot teachers and students.
We give up our children to the Internet and to the television
Let them babysit them;
We are too busy working for the almighty dollar

We don't even want to go to church anymore
We have arrived; we are now self-reliant
We are master of our own destiny, captain of our own ship

Who is this generation? This generation has no orientation
They entered the family unaccounted for
Where is home? Is it the church? Is it the school? Is it the street?
Is it the Internet? Is it the television?

Where can the children meet?
The walls are broken down, the lamps are getting dim
They need some more oil. We have plenty oil.
The question is who will take the time to pour it into the
lamp of the next generation to keep it from going out

Is this a generation without knowledge of the past
And no hope for the future
This generation lives for the moment
This generation tells themselves that they don't need anyone

This generation substitutes dope for hope
Some say forget the dope; just give me a piece of rope
Let me end what was not meant to be

This generation needs a new scope
This generation needs to know that there is hope in Christ Jesus.
Who is this generation?
This generation has no orientation.
They entered into the family through the back door,
With more troubles than John could write about.

What can I do to help this new generation…
This generation who is still 'Googling' for
The real meaning of life.

TIME

Time to pick up the pieces of what's left of your broken heart.
It's not too late to make a new start.

Time to shake the sadness.
Wash your face with the oil of gladness.

Time to open the window of your soul
Allow the Son to captivate your innermost being.

Time to walk in the fullness of time, quit looking back.
How can you get anywhere when you keep looking back?

Time to run like a bullet from a gun.
Leave confusion behind, it's not your job.

Run to the Fountain of Truth,
If you want to discover the fountain of your youthfulness.
Time to kill the desire of wanting to kill
Cain killed Abel, yet no one was able to kill him.

Time to tell you that a time is coming
When I will not be able to tell you that Jesus loves you
He died on the cross to save you
And that your riches will not get you into heaven.

As The Years Fly By

As the years go by I'm discovering who I am.
Who am I, you may ask?

I am a visionary. I look beyond the present.
I see the future the way it can be, if I have the wisdom
To understand That anyone who dares to try and change
The world to make it a Better place will suffer from
The backlash of the haters of peace and unity.

As the years go by, man, how they fly, yet it seems that time has
Stood still. To me it feels like nothing really ever changes, or
Should I say the more they change, the more they remain
The same.

Haters are still hating, lovers stop loving.
They blame it on the haters, say that
They are tired of loving.
Why must they continue to love and not
Be loved in return?

As the years go by, I'm discovering that the road to love and
Peace is to be at peace with yourself.
As the years go by, I find myself celebrating anniversaries of
Lies; the lies she tells have increased with
The advancement of technology.

As the years go by, I am learning that she will never change;
She likes to be the center of attention. She is like the
Eye in a Hurricane. Katrina has to take a back seat.
She is like the big Bad wolf; she makes it her quest to
Blow down the walls of trust and respect.

As the years go by, I am learning to understand that liars don't
Know how to be truthful; they invent lies. You don't have
To be Dead meat for them to spread their germs on you.
As the years go by, I am discovering that liars don't just lie
Because they want to; they tell lies to hide deep,
Dark secrets of self-hate and rejection.

IN THE EYES OF MYSELF

In the eyes of myself, I see myself.
I see beauty, joy, laughter, and pain.

I don't sit around and complain anymore.
I'm embracing the oneness I feel with myself.

I don't sit around and cry anymore. I am who I said I can be.
You are not responsible for my happiness.
I have joy, peace, and contentment that come
From God, the creator of the universe.

In your eyes I'm just a high school dropout. If it were up to you,
I would have been scraped from my mother's womb
And placed in a tomb
With the million other babies who never got the chance to
Be more than just a fetus.

In the eyes of myself, I am reminded that I have to be myself
If I want to leave *my* footprints in the sands of time.

Roots

You cannot have trees without roots. If you keep on
Moving from place to place, trying to find your roots, you
Will end up Like a Christmas trees with a short life span.

People will not see you for what you are.
All they will see are the ornaments that jingle on you. With a
Click of a switch, you are gone to the landfill of unwanted stuff.

Without trees, the earth would be a barren place.
Children with no roots are like a ticking time bomb.

This is what I beg of you: don't uproot your
Family without a good reason
If you feel it is necessary to uproot them, make sure to reroot
Them as soon as possible.
You cannot have trees without roots.

TODAY I DECLARE

Today I declare to the world that I will
Not bow out of the race of life.

Don't tell me what I used to be;
Tell me what I'm doing now.

Don't tell me what I can and cannot do;
You need to be quiet.
May I remind you that you are not the boss of me.

Don't tell me what you hear about me.
As long as you live, you will never understand me.

You are on a quest to bring me down,
But I will not allow you or anyone to bring me down.
Don't tell me who to be or not to be;
Let me be, so I can be.

WINTER BLUES

I dream of blue sky under an open heaven,
With milky white clouds drifting lazily
Across the warm Caribbean sea.

I dream of tourists from distant lands, walking on my white-
Sand beaches, leaving their footprints in the sands of time.

I dream of children building sandcastles on
The shores of my white-sand beach.

I dream of sweet reggae music being played by my countrymen,
While I rock my hips to the beat of their drums.

I dream of the tranquility of lying in a hammock between
The Coconut trees, letting the Jamaican sun melt my stress
Away, while the breeze from the ocean caresses my face.

Then, I open my eyes to the cold reality…
I am marooned in a snow castle
In a place call Iowa.

NOT WAITING

I am not waiting to exhale anymore;
I have found the way to the gold mine inside my head.

I am not waiting to exhale anymore;
I can see clearly now.
I'm not afraid anymore.

I am not waiting to exhale anymore;
I have found a way to be honest with myself.
I am at peace with myself.

I am not waiting to exhale anymore;
I am exploring new possibilities.
I now believe anything is possible.

I am not waiting to exhale anymore;
I am living each day as if it were the last day I have to live.

I am not waiting to exhale anymore;
I am not afraid of the voices in my head anymore.
I have accepted myself.
I am who I am.
I am not waiting to exhale anymore.

For Too Long

For too long I have given up so much of me
While doing for everyone else
And forgetting about myself.
Telling myself that I cannot be selfish.

So I gave and gave, till I became as hollow as a cave.
I was so busy doing for everyone
That I lost myself along the way.

Yesterday, I was forced to take stock of my life,
Only to discover that I was my own worst enemy.

So what will it profit me if I travel the pathway of life,
Worrying about what I don't have, while letting
My God-given gifts and talents go to waste?

Am I leaving my footprints in the sands of time?
How will the world remember me?

WHO

Who am I?
What am I?
I am not who you think I am

Why do you feel you have the right
To put me in the class of the no class?
I have beauty your naked eye cannot see!

Who am I?
What am I?

I am not afraid of trying
Not afraid of failing

I am not afraid of crying
No, I'm not afraid of dying

Who am I?
What am I?
I am a simple woman with extraordinary dreams.

COURAGE

Courage is not for the faint of heart
Not for the needing needy

Courage is priceless, it is worth
All the riches in the world

Yet you cannot buy it, if you don't have backbone
Courage will not come to your front door.

Courage walks with soldiers who are not afraid of fighting,
They will gladly die for what they believe in

How will you know if you have courage?
Be a voice to the voiceless
Courage speaks softly, yet it
Echoes across the globe

To All

To all the mothers who gave it all up
In order for your children to become something.
No one can hear our silent screams, you are screaming so loud,
Yet no one seems to hear, or even care.

To all the mothers who have been fired for calling off
Too many times, and end up in the soup line
While the dads are somewhere doing time,
Yet it feels like you are the one doing the time.

To all the mothers who work for minimum wage,
Do you sometimes cry yourself to sleep at night,
Wondering how to make ends meet?

You work so hard yet you are not able to make it on what you earn
Do you sometimes ask yourself what have you done
To be treated like you are the scum of the earth?

To all the mothers who are on the verge of giving up,
You are tired of being tired, tired of trying, tired of crying,
Tired of trying to open doors just to have them
Slammed shut in your face

You are not alone. Dry your tears and open the window of your soul
It's gonna be all right; please don't give up the fight.

QUEST

The quest to be
In a world of not to be
Makes you want to be
What you are not to be

Quick fix
Quick start
Quick answers to old questions

This will lead you from your quest to be

The quest to be
Is this something new
Wish I knew

All I know
I have a need to be what I want to be
In a world of not to be

Things My Grandmother Told Me

If everyone loves you, you have a problem

A problem so deep that you may need help
To rid yourself from the grip of self-destruction

A person who tries too hard to please everyone
Ends up hurting the ones they should be trying to please

Children are like slow cookers
It takes time to come to perfection

But you can rest assured that
Whatever you put in you will get out
Plus a little more

Don't try to be what you are not
If you do, you will never
Become who you were meant to be

Don't make promises you know
You cannot keep.

I Am Always Mindful

I'm always mindful to remember
The words of my dear grandmother

Show me your company
And I will tell you who you are
If you have too many friends,
You will be lonely

Wait for your turn
But don't lose your turn

If you pick up fire, you will get burned
Don't be a follower, be a leader
Know where you are coming from
Have a plan as to where you want to go

If you don't know where you are going
You are like a ship on the sea of life that has no destination
Your life will be an invitation to destruction.

Your eyes are the window to your soul
Be careful what you look at
After a while, you will start to see yourself in the eyes of the world.

YOU ARE

You are your child's role model.
You are the reason your child was born.
You are the first mirror your child looks through.

You are your child's role model.
Practice speaking kind words to your child

Love cannot be bought,
It must be taught.

You are your child's role model
Mold them with dignity and pride.
Teach your child to be kind and gentle.

You are your child's role model
If your children cannot be like you
Who will they be, what will they become?

A Place Called Home

Where is home?
For some, home is where the hurt is.

Mothers with black-and-blue eyes
Covered up with Revlon foundation
And wearing extra mascara to hide the sadness in their eyes.

Fathers are out all night getting high and dry.
The higher they get, the lower they feel.
Sad to say some don't even feel anymore.

God is the head of the family
He is the one with the answers to the problems facing the family.
How can He help when He is no longer welcome in the home?

CLASS OF THE CLASSES

Upper class
Middle class
Lower class
No class
High class
What is class
Where is class
Who is in the class
Who decides what class to put the class in
Upper class
Middle class
Lower class
No class
High class
Lower class is the bait for the upper class
The upper class will fight to the death
To keep the low class in the class of the no class
The middle class gets caught between the classes
While trying their best to sit in the high class.

WELFARE BABIES

I was fourteen years old when I got pregnant
Everyone believed it was a mistake

Getting pregnant was no mistake, I planned it.
That was my way of freeing myself from my parents' rules.

When you are fourteen
You tell yourself that your parent is dumb
They don't know what is hip
All they want to do is stand in the way of your happiness

Now I am twenty-seven years old, and a mother of four.
I woke up one morning only to find out
That I am now walking in my mother's shoes.
What do you know,
I am on my way to becoming a welfare grandmother.

THE GIRL

The girl who cried
Why did she cry?

Her sister had been killed, and she cried,
"Mi sister, mi sister"
"Mi big sister dead!"
"Mi sister, mi sister, mi big sister dead!"
"Whey mi a go do"

With pain ripping out her heart
She raised her hands and cried,
"Mi sister, mi sister, mi sister dead whey mi a go do".

She was not crying for police brutality
She was not seeking to kill the killer
She was crying for her sister, who was the pillar to her happiness.

What a mess.
The family nest no longer meshes
All she is feeling is distress
Her eyes were blinded with loving tears
Looking at her, I could not help my tears from falling
"Mi sister, mi big sister dead!"

My Daddy

My daddy and I don't see eye to eye, even though I wish we did.
I am not sure of the depth of his love;
Still I know his love for me will never change.
Chances are he will love me until his dying day.

There were days when I wondered about his love for me
I was too young to understand that so many things
Stand in the way of a father and daughter

Not just the laughter, I did not have his shoulder to cry on
Believe me, I was always crying
I was trying to understand why I was born
My heart would burn as it turned
The day will come when it will be my turn to run
Just like the bullet from a gun.

I did not get many hugs; there were bugs under the sheet,
Life for me was far from sweet; still I did not take to the street
I learned to sweep my feelings under the sheet
And to show my teeth.

My daddy and I don't see eye to eye
Now I think I know why.

BUSYBODY

The busiest people are the ones who have nothing to do
They are so busy doing nothing
They get in the way of those who have something to do.

They complain the most
Their pain is always worse
The bags of pain they carry
Not gaining the knowledge of knowing
That millions have done the same thing they are doing.

They were too busy wasting away their lives
On the street of complaining
They needed a compassionate companion
One who would share their pain in the bed of sorrow.

One who will borrow tomorrow's sorrows
And put it in today's wheelbarrow
Lend them two wings and like a sparrow
They will fly and sing of all their sorrows
The busiest people are the ones who have 'nothing to do'

PERFECT LIES

In the arms of someone else I did run, not that I wanted to
My life was a burden; I needed someone to tend to my garden.

My world was falling apart, I needed a new start.
Was this a part of living outside of one's self?
My life, I did place on a shelf

Only because I wanted to have you just the way you were,
Sometimes I ask myself why I allowed myself
To fall so deeply in love with you.

Now you love someone else.
While you are loving her, in the arms of someone else
I try to find myself, only to find out that
I was nothing but an empty shell, all because I sold myself short.

I feel like I am taking a shortcut to hell.
My friends keep telling me that I am smart,
I should try and make a new start.

Yet all I do is sit in the park
Trying to find a way to light my spark,
In the arms of someone else I am now running,
This time I am sure I will find myself.

LIFE

Life is filled with hugs and kisses,
Yet people are acting like bitches
And living like sons of witches

Swinging from personality to personality,
Refusing to face life's realty.

The youth's' in the inner cities still sinking
In the sea of Impossibility.
Every day this is their reality,
Many have lost their sanity.
Dear God, what a mess, everyone is crying, crying for stress.

Life is filled with guns, not to mention the drugs.
Who will sweep the blood and get it off the streets?

The youth's' tell themselves that life has no meaning,
They have no access; all they are getting is "what's left"
The meaning of success for them, it is on recess.

Dear God, what a mess, everyone is crying, crying for stress.
Life is filled with sadness
All I'm seeing is madness, there is no gladness.
Badness, nudeness,
And loudness seem to walk hand in hand in our land.

Love songs play every day;
Still hate travels from gate to gate.
I can't help but wonder what will be our fate.
Dear God, what a mess, everyone is crying, crying for stress.

Life, oh life, is this the way it should be?
My heart is faking and my world is shaking.
Tell me when this will cease, all I need is peace.
Dear God, what a mess, everyone is crying, crying for stress.

The Wrong Time

I was born at the wrong time for the right reason
They say I 'commit' treason because I came before my season

I entered time without a dime, the price of living I could not pay
So I started to pray, Lord, please don't make me a prey.

As I travel down life's lonely road, my load gets heavier
My friends become fewer,
Forever, they say, began yesterday

Too many questions, not enough answers.
For starters... like me, what shall I be?
I cease to be what others say I should be.

I learned too soon that when you are born at the wrong time
Many feel you should commit crimes,
Why should you
When the streets of life are paved with many different things

Don't wallow in self-pity, why allow yourself
To be stained with the sin of not achieving anything,

Don't you understand what it means
To be born at the wrong time for the right reason
Life is no treason; why don't you enjoy its season.

WHO AM I

Who am I when I don't know what I am?
The essence of life is not wrapped up in the color of one's skin

It is a sin to travel on life's sinking ship
Chipping away the value of my soul,

Who am I?

I am who I am when I know what I am,
Then I will not be wrong
Even though to others I was born wearing the wrong clothes.

To many, blackness is a shame
Yet they find it difficult to tame their white thoughts

Who am I?

Heaven help a black man who thinks he is white,
The black man will take care of the white man who spits
On his blackness,

When he begins to see himself as being equal with
the white Man, then he will not be wrong

Who am I?

Sing your song; listen to the sound of life.
You are who you are,
Even if you don't know who I am
What is your reality, can you see your destiny?
I don't believe in destiny,

Get to know your history
Then life will be no mystery
Who am I when I don't know what I am?

FEAR

I live in fear, I fear what I know, I know what I fear,
I am afraid of living, yet I don't want to die,
Should I not be afraid, how can I not fear?
All I see is blood paving the streets.

Someone once said that life is bitter and sweet,
All I am feeling is bitterness, where is the sweetness?

My grandmother told me if I live a good life,
When I die I would walk on the streets of gold,
She never told me that the hearts of men would be so cold
I know I will never live to grow old.

Bob Marley sings about "Trench Town Rock,"
On my block I can't turn my back
I will be shot even before I have the chance
To take up my schoolbook.

I watched in fear as gunmen cut my mother down
With bullets from their guns,
Mamma was pregnant; still they gunned her down,

I felt like someone was drowning me in a bucket of blood
When I saw the gunmen turn their guns on my little brother
And shoot him in the head.

Grandma, I wish you had told me
That Trench Town would be dripping with human blood,
Then I would have run like a bullet from a gun

Grandma, it is too late now,
Where would I run?
What's the use, Grandma?

I know what I fear, I fear what I know
The next bullet may be going through my head
Before you know it,
I will be dead,
I live in fear.

How Much More Blood

How much more blood can Mother Earth drink?
How many more bodies will she have to bury?
Do tell me please, how do you manage to drink so much blood?
Would you not rather drink the tears from your children's eyes
Who are so happy that they shed tears of
Joy playing with their Toys?

Can anyone tell me what is wrong with the people of this modern
World, can't they see that they are destroying their own selves?
Don't you wish you could do something
To stop these senseless killings?

I turn on my television, and what did I see,
Blood splashing across the screen, another businessman lay dead
Mother Earth, when will it end?
Mother Earth, he was a son of the soil,
Somewhere in the dark, a mother is crying for a son,
A wife is weeping for her husband,
Mother Earth, was he not a father?

What will we tell the children when they ask the question,
"Why did they kill our daddy?"
Mother Earth, tell me please, will you have to bury another body?
How much more blood can Mother Earth drink?

My Life

Did my life fall apart too soon?
You came into my life one rainy afternoon,
I placed my umbrella over your head
You ended up in my bed and you 'was' well fed.

You came with only the clothes on your back,
You are about to give me a heart attack,
Every day you sit on your lazy stool
Playing pool, waiting for your big break

My back is breaking from overwork
My responsibilities I cannot shirk.
You are acting like a jerk

You cannot be bothered to climb the ladder of success
All you are looking for is sweetness,
What a stress
Did my life fall apart too soon?

WHICH WAY

I don't know what to do
I wish I had a clue
All I know is I am feeling blue
This feeling sticks like glue
Sooner than later something must be done,
All I want to do is run.

How else will I get away from all my fears?
Sometimes I wonder if anyone cares,
My heart is tearing, yes, it is tearing

Life is teaching me all there is to know,
Still I am feeling low
The wind of fear is blowing,
Is it not showing that my senses are leaving me
Yet the memories keep haunting me
I don't know what to do,
Will someone give me a clue?

RIGHTS

Every man has the right to do what he wants to do,
No one should tell him what to do
He should be allowed to do the things that make him happy

To you I may be sloppy; does that mean I should be unhappy?
Even if I were a puppy, I'd still have the right
To be the puppy I want to be.

Every man should have the right to speak his truth,
As long as he can accept the truth that he makes mistakes too,

The time will come when he will do what others want him to do
When that time comes, he should do it
Only because he wants to do it
Every man should have the right to do what he wants to do,
As long as he can remember that he is his brother's keeper.

DEPRESSION

Many times I am depressed, I feel outnumbered
By the many problems I have to face
Oftentimes I am made to wonder
Will I find the strength to press on through?
Depression, discontentment, and discouragement

When you think about all those Ds, somehow you feel you
Are Destined for the dungeon of despair, life is not fair.

In this dungeon you will find many with disfigured faces,
It is so disgusting to be made to walk the corridors of those
Dark disgusting Ds—
Depression, discontentment, discouragement.

Good grief! It grieves me to know I am hurting like this;
The one time in my life when I am trying to be happy.
Happiness is a state of mind, they say,

Somehow, I feel even if I traveled to all the countries
In the entire World, I would not find peace of mind,
What a state to be in
Depression, discontentment, discouragement.

BURN THE BRIDGE

Burn the bridge that leads to sadness
Get rid of it
Don't sit under it

Life is not a burden; it is more like a garden.
In the garden of your life, let love grow,
Water it with the simple pleasures of life
Giving and taking all that you need to live.

If you sit on the bridge of happiness, your life will be a blessing,
Even if to others you are a curse,
What will you choose, to win or to lose?

Sometimes you must be all you want to be
Even if it means losing your best friend,
Burn the bridge that leads to sadness.

HUSH

Hush, America, hush, dry your weeping eyes,
You are strong, you are bold, you are brave
Hush, America, hush.
Hush, America, hush,
Sweet land of liberty,

Open your eyes to this new opportunity,
Let's rebuild your city
Hush, America, hush
Hush, America, hush,
Land of opportunity,

Land of possibility, the whole world looks to you for stability,
Martin Luther King was killed because he had a dream,
If he were here, you would hear him say, "Hush, America, hush."

CHOICE

You don't have to do what you don't want to do,
Do what you must do in order to be you,
You have the choice to be good or bad,
Your life is in your hands.

You can either join the reggae band or be the leader of a gang.
The voices you are hearing may be many,
Some are saying good things about themselves,
Nothing good they have to say about you.

You have the choice of believing in yourself,
Or deceiving yourself by thinking you are no good.
The choice is yours, do as you please,
As long as you can remember
That everyone was born free in a world of bondage.

Bond with your family and your friends,
Let them know that you love them.
The way to do this is to start loving yourself,
What will you choose?
You don't have to do what you don't want to do.

Good Morning

Did you stop to say "Good morning"
To someone this morning?

When you say hello to others,
It helps you to stay happy.

So look at it this way,
You are doing yourself a favor, when you say "Good morning"
Did you stop to say "Good morning" this morning?

WHAT WOULD I NOT GIVE

What would I not give to keep you near me?
I would be willing to give myself freely to you,
If you ask me to spent the rest of my life with you,
I would be the ink in your pen
Together we would write the stories of our lives.

What would I not give to make you truly happy?
Would I not climb the highest mountain to show you
How much I love you?
I would be more than willing to die for your love.

Your love is my bridge over troubled water.
Could it be that this world is getting colder every day,
And true love is still hard to find?
Am I not lucky to have your love?

Lonely are my days when you are not around,
Even though I know you will never take
Your precious love away from me.

I live for your love only, a kiss on the cheek, a warm embrace,
The look in your eyes speaks louder than a thousand voices
It echoes across the miles, making me smile.

Summer is hot, but not as hot as our melting pot full of love
Only a touch from you, and I melt like butter
Between a hot sunrise cocoa bread.

Could it be that you are the sun that ripens my mangoes
By multiplying my pleasure,
Would I not give all I have got so you never stop till I reach the top.

You are so sweet, when I am with you; I want to skip and hop
The vampire says this is love at first bite,
I say this is love at first sight.
What would I not give to keep you near me?

Signs Of The Times

Life is full of slime and crime, people acting like swines
Blaming it on de time, saying dem no have a dime
Yet dem a wine and dine an a sip red wine.

Wicked and wild sing the DJs with their rhyming words
Fooling de crowd, telling de youth dem fi bun more fire
While de government a fire, seh him no hab no money fi hire
Still de youth dem a bun more fire.

Some a pray bad praya, telling jah fi kill de killars
Still the higglers dem a run up on down cause de police dem a come
Wid dem gun fi shoot somebody down.

Some want de lawmen fi teck control,
Some only want to rock and roll.
In Rollington Town head a roll, mothers a groan cause dem a lose
Dem son to the bullets from de guns, de
Gun, de gun, de gun, de gun.

What a time, what a time, what a time, what a time
Mi tired a de crime, mi tired a de crime,
Mi tired a de crime, mi tired a de crime,

People heart get sour like lime Help me climb out a di slime
Help me climb out a di slime
Help me climb out a di slime Life is full of crime and slime
A time fi we tap acting like swines.

GREED

The seed of greed was planted yesterday, it is now our creed
Its fruit we eat, not being able to give thanks
Our heart is now a tank of thoughtlessness.
We like birds have lost our nest to the pest of restlessness,

A new breed of lawlessness we say is necessary
If ever we are going to make it big.

A wig we now wear, saying we don't care
Our clothes we will tear just to show them we don't care

What is there to fear? Poverty we will no longer bear.
No longer will we bear the shame of not having enough money
Have you not heard no money, no honey

Touch my money, and that will be the end of your honey.
We will be like bees on your head; you would wish you were dead

Because your children will not be able to eat bread
Your blood we will spread across the street
Just like the sheet on our bed
Did you not help to plant the seed of greed?

WHEN YOU ARE YOUNG

When you are young, free, and single
You tell yourself you must learn to mingle
At times you are caught in the middle of everything

When you are young, free, and single
You dance to every tune
Telling yourself it is too soon to act responsibly.
You never see the possibility of growing up
You feel that you have all the time in the world
To go round and round, making all kinds of sounds

You turn your head, but it could not go where you want it to go
What do you know, it is beginning to show
Your speech is slow; your feet refuse to go.
You no longer hear the songs of the birds
Your hair is white, where is your might

Your brightness is gone, the mourners are standing by
Where is your youthfulness?
It is gone; it slipped through your hands like a grain of sand
Now all you have is your memory bank

Are you still refusing to see
That you are no longer young, single and free?

NEWS

This is my view, I am afraid to watch the news
It shakes my nerves, it stays on my brain
Too many have been killed; the streets stink with stale blood

Yet, I can't make a wink because I may be thrown in a sink
With blood springing from my brain,
Another life has gone down the drain. Did anyone feel the pain?

Some blame it on the state of oppression the youth are facing
I will not fake it, I am not sure I will make it
One of the dons may shoot me in my head
And if by some miracle I don't die on the spot

You can bet your bottom dollar
If they take me to kick the pig in his head
Kingston Public Hospital (KPH)
I will wake up in the arms of the undertaker.

I will be forced to meet my maker
What will I tell Him
When I never get the chance to know Him
To me, to live is hell and to die is to face another hell

While politicians sing and the church bell rings
Another soul has been cast in a burning hell or living hell
This is my view, I am afraid to watch the news.

I WOULD BE A HERO

I would be a hero of the downside of life,
If I should act upon what I got from life

To be an unwanted child moving from hand to hand.
What did I get from the womb of time? Sour lime.

To others this is a crime, so they sit back until
They slip on their own slime, then they blame it on the time.

Lest you forget, we all got sour lime from the womb of time
It comes in the form of a generational curse
What do you have to say for yourself?
I would be a hero of the downside of life.

KISS MI NECK

Kiss mi neckside wey mi plate a lasco mackerel an rice
Tell mi who nyam mi hat, hat plate a lasco mackerel an rice

Mi sure sey yu mout nor yu tongue neva get di chance fi
Tase de sweetness an di wetness a mi plate
A hot lasco mackerel an rice.

Feel mi hart, tel mi sey mi ded cause everyting look red
Tell mi anyting but no tell mi sey a di dread
Nyam mi plate a lasco mackerel an rice.

Mi naah mek no mountain outa no mole hill
Cause a hole heap a rice mi lef inna mi plate

God bles di day wen mi granny did sen mi
Go a school fi larn fi rite pon slate
Now mi travel fram state to state wid mi
Plate a lasco mackerel an rice.

Mi git up outa bed before cock crow an tek
Up mi hoe fi go chopup Mass Joe

So you tink sey a joke mi dida mek if a
Did ketch I'm you woulda hear

Wey you sey if a food mi a cuss ova so
You neva hear sey man sell dem
Birt rite fi pece a cheese
So mi hab di rite fi cuss ova mi lasco mackerel an rice.

Teck mi pot roast, teck mi chicken, teck mi
Ram goat you can even curry di rope

But tap! how yu hab so much mout?
A hab a feeling sey yu help nyam
Mi plate a lasco mackerel an rice

But if yu tink sey yu bad si a pud dung mi jug
A pure bulk syrup come teck a sop no.

Kiss mi nekside a no Mass Joe dawge dat
Wid mi pat a lasco mackerel an rice

Feel mi hart tel mi anyting tel mi sey mi ded
But no tel mi sey de dawg gan wid
Mi pat a lasco mackerel an rice
Kiss mi nekside a wey dis pon mi tiday.

THE PAST

The past is the future
The present is its teacher
Tell that to the preacher
Let it teach you the way of life

Be rich in your spirit, then learn to share it
Hold no writ against your brother

Labor in love and stay above the whisper of hate.
For the sake of your children, watch and pray
If you don't, Satan will use them as prey

The cycle of hate will circulate
Like coffee it will percolate
All who drink from the cup of hate will retaliate.

You will find yourself standing at the gate of life
Before you know it, the past will be your future.

So Many

So many with sad faces, smiling through their fears,
So many with tired eyes, their bodies are too weak to complain,
To them there is nothing to gain, so they never share their pain.

Some people look happy, but if you look beyond their laughter,
You will see their tears,
Many are like puppets being dragged from place to place
Trying to find a palace that does not exist,
Wearing cheap expensive clothes.

Some people are like dust, they will sit and rust
If no one dusts them with a puff,
Some people still act like scruff, not because it is a must.
Some people never learn to trust themselves,
How will they learn to trust anyone, only God can tell.

Some people will never know that there is more to life
Than what meets the eye, I am no expert
I will ring no bell of knowledge; I never went to college

I too have to face life's challenges,
Some people will never overcome
Because they never ask God for courage
That is why there are so many sad faces.

MAYBE

He said maybe he would love me when he stops loving her
I was trying to be a hero, so I stayed with him
When we made love, if that is what it was
In the middle of lovemaking he held me close, real close

I closed my eyes and opened my ears
My body gave way to his gentle caressing,
He then kissed me with all his strength
Then he called her name. I responded to
Him even though I know I will never win

Because he will never stop loving her
Maybe one day he will accept me
Maybe she will come back, and I will have to step back
For now I am going in his tract

His feelings for me are like a burden on my back
That gets heavier day by day
Still I am waiting for my payday
Maybe one day he will stop loving her and start loving me.

Determined To Win

I have a part to play in this great race of life
I know where I am going; there is no doubt in my mind
Looking back at yesterday gives me the courage to face tomorrow
What must I do today with all its questions without answers.

There comes a time in everyone's life
When you will have to face this daring world
Face it with boldness, forget the coldness
Be determined you can make it to the top.

Maybe I am not the Bright Star
I know I have many scars
Sometimes I sit and cry a river of tears
My tears will never fall in vain

The pain I am feeling is helping me to grow.
It may not show, but still I am growing and learning to shine,
The darker it gets, the brighter I will shine
I will outshine the darkness in my life
Can't you see I was born to win?

His Vessel

Do you want to be possessed by the power of God?
He told me He will give me the strength to do the impossible
I want to be a portable vessel
Portraying the image of the unstoppable,
Unforgettable God.

Use His words to guard your mind
Mend your ways by giving way to the spirit of life
If you do, your light will shine bright
Resist the devil, and he will flee

Remember, he is nothing but a flea.
'he' will try to fill you with fear
You have nothing to fear because Jesus is always standing near
Give Him all your cares; to Him you are very dear

He will help you bear your heavy load,
As you travel life's lonely road
Be a vessel of honor each and every hour
Then you will be possessed by the power of God.

WHO WILL

Who will care for the homeless who are living in distress?
She sits in a corner outside the building of knowledge
No one acknowledges her,
To many she is just an old lady.
Where are her children? Where is her family?
She is sitting at the door of insanity in the middle of the second city

I can't help but wonder!
Was she one of the street people they dumped in St. Elizabeth
Like garbage at Riverton City.
They say the hand that rocks the cradle rules the world
I don't know where she is from
Did she do something wrong?

What difference does it make?
Who will give a dime?
Who will spend some time to reach this old lady in time?
Will the government care? How about the opposition leader?
I guess they are too busy with who is responsible for the murders
In Tivoli Gardens.

The question is still being asked! Who will care for the Homeless?
Not me, I have to go to school
I'm too busy with the affairs of the country to interfere

My hands are full, don't you know crime is on the increase
Business is increasing; I'll pay to carry her to Riverton City Dump
I will see to it that they take her on a day
When they are burning rubbish.

If she is still alive after we finish our all-island crusade
Our outreach committee will hold a
Meeting to see what can be done
For now all we can do is pray for her.

Who will care for the homeless who are
Sitting under the table of society?
Like Lazarus they are begging for the crumbs of compassion
It is time for us to stop giving lip service

TRIBUTE TO SEPTYMUS WHITE

Papa, you never failed to show me love. Nothing you had was ever too good for you to give me. I respected you in every way. As a child growing up in your house, you always made sure I got whatsoever was available. I remember the days when money was scarce; not that it is any better now. You and Mama would give me the last five cents you had to your name and send me to school, while your children stayed home.

Why did you allow that to happen? You used to say you didn't want anyone to say 'because I was not your child'. Why didn't you send yours and leave me behind? It is because of the way you treated me, that I have learned how to be a good mother to my children.

Papa, you were the first person who taught me how to meditate. You used to say to me, "Yvonne, the month in which you are born, no one will be able to harm you or keep you down. People will try to push you down. Yvonne, don't be afraid of anyone. You must find a way to bounce back." I was too young to understand the meaning of what you said, so I used to close my eyes and try to understand the meaning of your words.

I have been pushed down several times; still being pushed, but never to the ground. I have always found a way to bounce back up, and because of that, I never get into a quarrel with anyone. You have taught me to use my mental strength to find a way instead of fighting.

Papa, you were not perfect, but I see the way some fathers treat their children; if asked to rate you as a father, I would give you an 'A'. If you were able to do so much with so little, who and what can stop us from achieving greatness?

Papa, you did what you could. Now you can rest your weary head because you are not dead. You are alive and well in your children, and in their children. They will keep your light burning bright.

TICK TOCK

Tick tock goes the clock sitting on a rock
While the world rocks on in sin and shame, feeling great pain,
Still Christians playing games, gambling with the souls of men,
Sipping champagne in their den. Many cease to pray,
Giving room to The evil one to prey on the weak

Meekness is not weakness, where is your inner strength
Can't you smell the stench from the decaying flesh of men?
Where are the weeping mothers? Where have the watchmen gone?
Time is slipping away, awake from your slumber
The day is far gone

Night cloud is falling, the savior is calling,
Still millions are falling.
Fame and fortune many seek, to them it is very sweet
While Christians sleep and Satan sweeps through the hearts of men

Bitterness becomes sweetness, holiness
Seems to be a thing of the past
Beauty now walks from outside in,
Satan will sit and grin, saying he is going to win

The hands of time are slipping,
Christians, please awake and proclaim the word of God
From state to state before it is too late
Tick tock goes the clock, please don't look back.

JAMAICA

Jamaica, the land of sugar and rum,
The place where the reggae beat is never done,
A land of sunshine, wood, and water,
A place where every man loves his mannish water, and his daughter.

I journeyed to Dunn's River Falls where I like to see one and all,
The tourists from America, Japan, and Siberia,
I even saw the men and women from Liberia.

I thought it would be fun to check the south coast,
So I journeyed to Invercauld. There they showed me Lover's
Leap, YS Falls, Apple Valley Park, and Bamboo Avenue.
And you know what, I liked the venue. They made me
Appreciate that the joys of nature are never too late.

How could I forget to take you up the Black River and give you
A piece of ram goat liver? The lovely watermelon, mango, and
Pear and the sweet, sweet Jamaican ginger beer. The luscious
Jamaican bammy and fish; How could I forget the national dish?

Blend them together with the deep blue sea,
And the people with their warm hospitality.
Preserve our environment; I am begging you please,
For if you destroy it, I will give you no ease,
Jamaica, the land where we all know
The sun's rays will always glow.

PEACEMAKER

It brings more joy to be at peace than to be at war.
Words of hate spread near and far,
Follow your heart; come let's make a new start.

Have you not heard that true love is to be at peace with yourself?
Children of God are blessed peacemakers. How
About spreading the fire of peace.

Send your enemy a gift of love; rise up from your bed of hate,
Take a break; it is not too late to leave it at the gate.
Fan the flame of love; send it to the sick and lame.
Let it tame the Crazy and heal the lazy.

To be a peacemaker, you must stay in the vine; in a little while
You will be serving new wine. Don't try to be like the rest, for
God will Detest. When he does, the tempest will blow and
Words of hate will flow.

A peacemaker is a preserver. Like the angels, you too must say,
"Let There be Peace on Earth, and let it begin with me"
Put on the cloak of peace and let love flow wherever you go.
To be a peacemaker, let folly stay down the valley. If you
Die trying to make peace, you will never be afraid of the
Valley of death

I know it is hard to be a peacemaker,
Learn to bear the pain, for wisdom you will gain.
It is the break of a brand-new day. Let us break the chain of hate.

Come let us bake the cake of peace,
Teach us, Lord, to sit at the gate of mercy
As we learn to see each man for who he is
And not who we think he should be.

Let us tear down the banner of hate, help
To break the bread of peace
The words of God give you the right to become troubleshooters,
Take up your guns and shoot words of love.

Let us all keep the fire of love burning brighter
It is not the will of God to let your eyes burn with the smoke
Of hate, take a plate and serve the message of peace.
Let us eat before it is too late.

Peace, perfect peace,
Let it rest in peace, then the war will cease.
Have you not heard that true love is to be at peace with yourself?
It brings more joy to be at peace than to be at war.

KIDZ

Kids today are living in a daze,
They use words we could never use or say,
Kids today are living in fear. For many, life is far from gay
Some even call it a day, before they reach their night.

What can I say; they are experiencing a living hell,
No one seems to be able to tell,
Kids today hide themselves in a shell,
Bells are ringing, songs they are singing,
Yet they are sinking in deep despair
To them no one seems to care, so they never learn to share.

What do they do? Rebel! Rebel!
How do I know? Wish I knew
All I know is I feel their pain

Many think it is nothing,
For me it is like a grain of sand in my eye that will not go away.
Kids today are sinking in deep despair,
They are trapped in a world of fantasy,
They have no stability; they are searching for security,
This is a sad reality; kids today are living in a daze.

MIND GAME

W hen your mind is sick
And your heart is heavy
And it feels like you are carrying
The weight of the whole world on your shoulders

Should you listen to the people around you
Who tell you to pull over on the soft shoulder
And take you medication?
It will make you feel better.

No, I don't need any medication. Why are you trying to
Trick me? Everybody knows that if I take the medication,
It will trap me and turn me into a pill popper.

Wish you would all leave me alone so I can smoke and
Meditate. I want to climb on the smoke from my pipe,
Like Jack and the Beanstalk
I'm trying to find that golden egg,
But all I'm hearing is your voice in my head saying "Take PTO."

LIP SERVICE

You think they care about your welfare,
What does it matter if they say they care,
Yet act as if they don't care.

You care for them in a funny way,
Frankly, you are more concerned about your pets
And who is going to win some stupid bet
Than those children living in poverty.

Have you ever stopped to think that one day the
Tables may turn, when the cows come home to roost
And you lose your economic boost.
What will you do when at last your butter refuses to churn?

FACES

Which face are you wearing?
Who are you today?
Do you even know who you want to be tomorrow?

Will you be the scary clown walking around town,
Or will you be a faceless person lost in a crowd of wannabes?

Which face will you go to confession with?
Are you a witch, the white witch of Rose Hall,
The lady who had a ball killing all of her many husbands?
Her spirit, they say, still roams about
In Rose Hall, Montego Bay, in the island of Jamaica.

Whose face will you wear when you have to face
The Maker of all faces?

Your face is not your own, it belongs to The One
Who said, "Let there be...," and so it was. The Almighty God
And the Holy One who breathed His breath of life into our nose
And gave us legs to walk on,
The One whose name everlasting life came from
Life is not a game; God knows your name.

BUILDERS

We are all builders in our own way,
Some build castles, some high-rise buildings
Some build walls to divide, some build
Bridges that bring people Together.

I, myself, have a lot of chips on my shoulder. I'm not daring
Anyone to knock them off. I'm adding them to my 'pie of
Understanding'. I will bake it and share it with all who will listen.

I was born at the wrong time for the right reason.
I'm not looking for answers; I'm part of the answer.

I am pregnant with words, and my head water just broke
From the turmoil and unrest that is taking place in the world.

Law and order without human dignity will never solve the
Problems of humanity, why create more calamity.
Please don't burn down the bridges built on the backs of slaves

When all is said and done, I would rather be a silent hero
Than a spit bomber who is about to create a
Tsunami in the process of becoming a self-made god.
We are all builders; what are you building?

ANGER

Anger rests in the heart of a fool
My granny never raised 'no' fool,
So I will keep on reminding myself that one day,
I too will stand tall at the boarder of injustice.

I will declare to all who will listen.
I refuse to allow anyone to label me.

I'm tired of you talking *about* me instead of talking *to* me.
Because you tell yourself that I'm a fool,
You want to use me like a tool
While expecting me to stay cool.

Your empty promises are like winter in the middle of summer
And summer when it is winter.
Don't be a twentieth century Samson. Stop being so angry.

Listen to the voice of the people; they are expecting change,
Not chains.
Why are you trying to put a lock on the mouth
Of freedom? Better is a stranger who tells you the truth, than
A friend who pats you on your back and tells you that all is well
When deep down, they know that you are far from doing well.

How

How will you know what you know
When you don't know what you know?

Some say that life is no joke; this is why they stand in
Line to see the Pope, hoping that by looking at his Holy
Face, they will see the light at the end of the tunnel.

Let go of the rope of hate, find hope in knowing that
There is a God who cares. His love will reach
You no matter how far away you are.

Let it be known to one and all
That God visits the drug houses and the bars,
He knows where you are
He knows when you are drunk.

You may be able to hide the needle marks all over
Your body from your family and friends,
But you cannot hide from the eyes of the Almighty God.

He has the master key to our heart, He will help you
Make a new start. Find hope in knowing that He is
Waiting for you to drink from His fountain of love.

LEARNING, LEARNING

I'm learning to step back without looking back,
I'm holding on to what I know,
The million-dollar question is what do I know?

Like Joseph, I too have dreams. I dream of doing for my children
What no one did for me, giving them roots. How will I give them
Roots when I keep stepping on sinking sand?

Joseph told everyone and anyone who would listen about his
Dreams. My dreams are locked away deep inside the corners of
My heart and on pieces of paper stuck up in a box somewhere,
Waiting to be shared with someone somewhere
Who is shedding tears of hopelessness, while here I'm
Wrestling with the thoughts of hopelessness,

Joseph was set up to pull some people up. God is reminding
Me not to get upset and depressed when things don't go
The way I planned.
Your prison is not meant to break you,
But to shape you and mold you into His image.

FATHER OF LIFE

Father of life, I worship You
With You by my side, I can
Ride the tides,

I will not allow anyone to tie me down,
I will abide by Your side,

Father of Creation, I raise my voice
To sing Your praise

Because of You, I have a song
In my heart,

Father of Creation, You mean
The world to me,

You are my mother, You are my father
You are my sister and my brother,
You are my doctor and my healer,
Father of all Fathers, where would I be without You?

BROKEN

Broken, broken dreams,
My dreams are broken, few words are spoken,
Where can I find a token to put into the lottery of life

Chaos to change the course of unfulfilled dreams
Why am I depressed? Do I have enough to
Last me for the rest of my day?

I have food; need some clothes that can wait,
Have fifty cents in my bank account,
How will I meet my needs, I'm not talking about greed,
Children depending on me with my daily needs,
Packed with millions of selfish greed.

Where do I belong, seems like the deck is stacked against me
Sometimes I ask myself why me,
Then I hear a small voice inside my head saying
Trials come to make you strong,
Then I find myself asking how strong do I need to be!

MIND GLITCH

Please don't ask me what I know
If you do, I will be the first to tell you
That I don't know, yes I really don't know,
And what I know, I don't even know if I know anymore

Why did you turn your back on me, tell me, won't you tell me
Please, I'm begging you, where must I go?
Who must I turn to, to find myself?

I'm lost in a maze, I'm in a daze
Everything looking hazy, some try to tell me
That I'm going crazy,

I see people following me,
Every time I leave my house, they come following me,
Then everybody tells me that I'm seeing things, but
Deep in my heart I know what I'm seeing

They don't believe me,
They look at me as if I'm going out of my mind.
Out of my mind, I'm out of my mind, out
Of my mind, I'm out of my mind,
Am I going crazy, can someone tell me please,
Am I going crazy?

I'm lost in a maze; I live in a daze,
Everything looking hazy, I'm tired of people
Telling me that I'm acting crazy,

They don't see what I'm seeing
You don't feel what I'm feeling
Sometimes I wanna get so far,

I wanna run, run so far away,
But where, where must I run,
Where, oh, where must I run,

Everywhere I go, I see faces in the clouds,
Yes, I see faces in the clouds,
But nobody believes me,
They all think that I'm going crazy,

Sometimes I think I am, and that is when I feel like dying,
Feel like I don't even want to live anymore,
Nobody believes me,
They don't even understand what I'm going through,
No, they don't even believe me,
They think I'm going out of my mind.

I see faces in the clouds; I hear voices in my head,
I see people following me everywhere I go,
Tell me what to do, I know I'm not crazy,

I'm not losing my mind, no, no, I just want to get away,
Yes, I just want to get away from these voices in my head,
If I close my eyes, will I see their faces,
Will they still follow me?

Can someone tell me what they want from me,
What did I do, why do you keep following me?
Do you think I'm a Pokémon?
Why are you trying to find me?

Everywhere I go, you keep hunting me like I'm an outlaw,
Talking about the law, they don't even believe me,
I'm tired of calling and telling them to stop
These people from following me,
But they don't even believe me,

No, they don't, nobody believes me,
Why don't they believe me?
Do they all think that I'm losing my mind?
Why can't you believe me?
Tell me why, tell me why.

WHEN YOU ARE TIRED

When you are tired of fighting and
Tired of getting knocked down
Learn to lie down and pretend that it is over.
While the enemy is celebrating, use that time to refocus,
Use your inner strength to fight, fight like hell, fight, fight,

There is no place in the world for cowards,
Shake yourself up, hold on to your faith,
You can do all things through Christ, who gives you strength.

To be a champion, you must learn how to take the beating,
From the people who make it their quest to label you
By demeaning you as they try to take away your self-worth.
Don't you ever allow them to scare you.

Character is not measured by how much
Money you have, the car you drive,
Where you live, or what school you went to,
Don't you dare roll over and play dead.

Use your head; think twice before you answer your enemies.
They have money and power, yet they spend all their
Waking hours trying to take candy from a baby.

DON'T

Don't waste your time complaining
About what people did to you or did not do for you,
Rise above the pain, build yourself an ark.

Don't allow yourself to be carried away in the wave of rejection.
Learn to inject yourself with the knowledge of
Knowing who you are and whose you are.

I find peace in knowing that my heavenly Father loves me,
If I didn't feel His loving arms around me,
Comforting me, I would be a total mess

He doesn't take my problems away
He is helping me to understand that my
Troubles don't come to break me,
They are meant to *make* me.

STILL

Still trying to understand the reason behind the madness of
People who spend their lives searching for happiness in places of
Sadness. They invent evil intentions, trying to get attention.

In their quest for happiness, they invite confusion and bitterness,
Then they turn around and blame the world for all their troubles.

Sadness is more than a state of mind. It runs in the
Bloodline, just like blood flowing through your veins

Learn to clean the corners of your heart because
Out of the heart flows life. Please don't clog it
Up with plaques of hate and resentment

Teach your heart to be content by embracing the facts of
Life. You have no control over what people do or say. Work
On the words that flow from your heart. The Bible tells us
That out of the abundance of the heart the mouth speaks.

A stable heart is a treasure; take care of your heart. That is
The best way to avoid madness and embrace happiness.

SELF-WILL

I am sure things are going to be fine,
I am sure all is going to be okay
I am confident about tomorrow
I am not afraid to try.

I am willing to start over again,
I am a strong woman
I am not alone
I will not take the blame

I know what I want out of life
I promise myself to be happy
I will do my best to help myself
I will never allow myself to be used,
I shall live life to its fullest
I will continue to believe in God
I will never give up on life

I am never alone
I am a homemaker
I create visions
I am an optimist
No one is going to push me around
Don't you ever try to get me out

STAY TRUE

Because of my grandmother, I can keep my head above the
Waters of disappointments in my life.

I will allow nothing or no one to break me.
I am what I am, yes; I know that I'm different,
I have been told many times to trade my values for what is trendy.

I will admit to you that at times I'm tempted
To give in to the pressures.
Why not bend a little?
If you would, life would be a little easier,
What do you have to lose?

Then, I find myself praying and calling out to my
Heavenly Father to help me make it to the next day.

Then the Holy Spirit sings a song of comfort to me.
At times I can almost feel His breath on my back
And His arms around my shoulder,
Telling me everything is going to be okay if I keep my eyes on Jesus!

LET YOUR TEARS

Let your tears be your Voice,
When you are too weak to speak.

Your mother's love, your mother's hug,
Will carry you when you are too weak to carry yourself.

Tears are emotions
That will travel over
The ocean of time.

Emotion is like lotion.
Use the lotion of sympathy
To reach out to help
Meet the needs of those in need of help.

EMOTION

If you have a heart that beats and eyes to see
You will never be able to sweep away
The emotion you feel when you watch
A mother hug her sons that she thought were killed
By the unending violence in Sudan.

I'm reminded of a verse in the Bible
That tells us that God bottles up our tears,
Hush, Mama, hush
Cry if you must.

Yes, I cannot even begin to understand
The pain you are feeling,
From having your children ripped
From your loving arms.

There is no stronger love than a mother's love.
Her love will rock you to sleep at night,
Even as machine guns light up the night sky
As you ask the God (you don't know) "Why?"
Go ahead and cry.

IF

If things were different, I would be different
If things were better, I would be better off.
If we can't communicate, please don't hate me if I leave.
If you abuse me, don't be surprised if I become an abuser
If you smile with me, I will smile back at you.
If you show me respect, I will give it back to you.
If you give me your time, I will spend mine with you.

If you trust me, I may learn how to trust you too.
If you look after me, I will look after you
If you are honest with me, I can't promise you I will be at all times!
If you love me enough to give me some space,
I won't be afraid to make space for you.

If you stop complaining about me and talk to me,
Then I would tell you why I do the things I do.
If you deceive me, don't blame me if I do the same to you.
If you stop to look in the mirror, you will see the log in your eye
Then I am sure you will not spend so much time trying to
Take the speck out of mine.

If you feel unwanted and unloved, don't be afraid to
Spend time with Yourself. If you begin to love yourself,
You may be surprised to know, I love you too.
If we can be comfortable with whom we are,
There would be no need for *ifs*.

MOMMY, PLEASE ANSWER ME

*M*ommy, why do birds sing?
They sing because they cannot talk.
Mommy, where is my daddy?
Honey, your daddy is in prison.

Mommy, what is prison?
It is a place to keep bad people.
Will my brother go to prison too?

Mommy, who made the world?
No one, it just evolved.
What does it mean to evolve?
Child, I really don't know
I guess it means that God was involved.

Mommy, why is your skin white and my skin black?
What does the N-word mean?
Is it like the F-word?
Will you put soap in my mouth if I say it?

Mommy, you need to get a very, very big bottle of soap for
Grandma's mouth. She calls me the N-word all the time.

Mommy, can you give me something to drink to make
My skin look like yours?
Why?
So Grandma will love me like she loves my other cousins.
Mommy, why don't you let me go visit my other grandmother?

I wish I had magic powers
If I did, I would wave a magic wand and turn Grandma into me,
Then I would be her,
Why?
I would treat her the same way she treats me
Then she would know how it feels when
People call you the N-word.

YOU ARE

You are trying to see me go down
Telling wicked lies on me
You are unable to sleep
Because of your schemes

I'm not a schemer
However, I will remain a dreamer
My dreams are big
Even though I remain small

Smiling to myself as I push ahead
My head I will use to get ahead
Holding on to the words of wisdom

I was told to walk the way a woman should,
Or the way you think they should
What if I don't?

If you mess with me
You are messing with my children,
Why are you trying to bring me down?

You Will

If I can, you will
Life was never meant to be easy

Pick up the pieces of your life
And fight with all your might

If I can, you will
Maybe you are feeling alone

It is okay to be alone
Being alone will help you to understand
Life in a new light
If I can, you will

WOMAN

Woman, some say woe to man
Woman of beauty bearing in sorrow

You are brave, you are proud
You are one of the proud mothers of creation
Carrying the cares of the children you bear

Strong woman, brave woman
You are not afraid of anything
You work very hard for your living
Yet you find time to play with your children

You never stop praying
Everything around you is falling apart
Yet you find a way to keep your children happy and safe

Many times you are abused by those around
They tell wicked lies about you to see if they can break your spirit

If only they knew that you are like the River Pishon
Which runs in the belly of Africa
Where you find rare and precious gold.
I am a black woman, I will not step back
Because I was the first to teach you what love was all about.

BREATHE

Don't worry, don't hurry
Learn to take life in stride
If you do, you will have no need
To hide from the storms of life

Don't worry, stop for a while and huddle,
If you do, you will not be bothered
By the puddles of unforetold delays

Don't worry, don't hurry
No need to live your life by the wayside of unfulfilled dreams
Eat a bowl of ice cream; don't allow anyone to cream you,

Dream big, laugh loud, be bold
If you do, your eyes will behold
The beauty in the ugly that life dumps on you,
Pump water from the well of understanding,

Stand up for what you believe in,
Stop and breathe, live in the now

Don't hold your breath in,
While you try to reverse time,
The good old time and the good old days
Don't need you to hang on to them.

SAY WHAT

Grandma had a barn with six cows that laid eggs,
Five chickens that mooed like cows
And a goat that wore a coat made of chicken skin
While the family dog spent all day yawing instead of barking

Grandpa had a pipe that he used to drink milk
Whenever Grandma try to talk to him, he started to yawn

Grandma went to the pawnshop to pawn her wedding ring,
When all of a sudden the ring started to sing,
And she took off her wig to see what pig was texting in her head
Grandma started to yawn then said, "It's time for me to go to bed."

SOMETIMES

Sometimes the sad times become the glad times.
Sometimes bad times become the good times.

Sometimes the weak ones become the strong ones.
Sometimes we tell ourselves we can't make it,
When the truth is we are making it.

Sometimes we find ourselves lost in the maze of life
Sometimes we become lost within ourselves

Sometimes the world is waiting on us.
To prove to ourselves that we can be ourselves,

Sometimes I am waiting on you to show me you believe in me.
Sometimes we are just afraid of failing
Sometimes we just want to feel welcome.

Sometimes I just want to say I'm sorry without you judging me,
Sometimes I need a shoulder to cry on.
Sometimes I need my children to show me they still love me.

Sometimes I need my father and mother to believe in me,
And the truth is most times I would be happy
Just to know you are happy.

THE SOUND OF LAUGHTER

To laugh is to live
To have peace of mind in the midst of chaos

Laughter is anti-wrinkle cream
To laugh is to live, embracing each moment
With love and understanding

Laugh and spread sunshine on cloudy days
Laughter is the grease that keeps the
Wheel of time running smooth

Without laughter, there would be no life after,
To laugh is to empower one's self to face
The troubles that come knocking at our doors,

So go ahead, permission is granted, laugh till you
Cry, and laugh even when you are crying
Laughter is the answer to the call for happiness

Go ahead, build your barn
Fill it with laughter
Laugh, laugh, laugh

WHAT TIME IS IT?

Time to pick up the pieces of what's left of your broken heart.
It's not too late to start over,
Time to shake the sadness.

Wash your face with the oil of gladness
Time to open the window of your soul,
Allow the Son to captivate your innermost being.

Time to walk in the fullness of time
Quit looking back. How can you get anywhere
When you keep looking back?

Time to run like a bullet from a gun,
Leave the confusion behind
It's not your job.

Run to the fountain of truth,
If you want to discover the fountain of your youth.
Time to kill…
To kill the desire of wanting to kill.

WHAT'S WRONG

What does it mean to forgive? For this reason I truly must live
For only this reason I strive to live,
For to live is to give; for this reason I was born
For without forgiveness there would be no heaven

For often I wonder why not eleven disciples,
For maybe if He only had eleven there would be no need
For Judas to sell him out for thirty pieces of silver

For what reason did Peter deny Him,
For I'm trying to understand
Why King Herod wanted to kill Jesus when he was a baby.

For what reason do people kill people
For I'm still searching to a find out
Why fathers leave their family

For if you can tell me what is wrong with the world,
Without the fear of not truly knowing
Then I would say you are what's wrong with the world

For I'm here to tell you that I am what's wrong with the world,
You are what's wrong with the world,
They are what's wrong with world,
For we all are what's wrong with the world.

ADDICTION

Addiction is no joke,
Living for dope is not a hoax,
Addiction will lead you on a path of no return,

Drugs will take you by the arm
And whisper in your ear how much he loves you,
When the plain truth is he wants to
Rob you of
Your self-esteem.

Life as it was meant to be, shall no longer be
For a sniff of coke you will choke your mother
If she stands in your way, preventing you
From reaching your Highness.

Addiction changes your personality
And takes you away from reality.
It will dump you on the highway of insanity.

Yes, my friend, drugs will lead you on the pathway of madness
Then leave you in the valley of sadness,
While he undresses you and takes away your human dignity,
And exchange it with alternative facts.

They say you cannot judge a person
Unless you walk in their shoes.
I'm not judging you,
I'm only telling you what I'm seeing.

Addiction has no class barrier,
He doesn't care if you are white or black or purple,
Rich, poor, fat, skinny, or lazy,

When you are an addict, you tell yourself that you are the president,
Believing that you can lie your way out of telling lies
Anyone who tries to stop your highness is in danger
This is not a hyperbole,
There are no alternative facts.

Move On

When it is gone, move on
Stop listening to the voices inside your head,
Who want to see you dead, use your head,
Quit doing things the same way while expecting a different result

Gladness sometimes shows up in a package of sadness,
Learn to laugh at yourself
Don't look at everything so seriously.

Satan comes to kill, steal, and destroy,
Ultimately you have the last say
It is not what they say about you,
It is how you react to what they say.

Everyone knows how to talk
Few learn how to listen,
Be one of the few.
If you learn how to listen to your own heart,
You will become your own bright spark,
When it is gone, move on.

COULD IT

Could it be that the world and its inhabitants are in turmoil?
Some say, to the victor goes the spoils.
Now it is the oil, this new pipeline going across the Indian land,
Can the tribe stop the pipeline? Who will take the bribe?

Could it be that Indians have a blind trust no one can break down?
Are they willing to lay down their lives to live for what
They believe or will they give in to the threats of death
And destruction?

Could it be that we are not able to come to a conclusion,
And there is going to be a revolution,
Martin Luther King would still be alive
If he had shut his mouth,
When they told him to.

Better to be a dead hero,
Than a walking dead
And no wisdom in your head,
Sleeping on someone else's bed.

As

As the years go by, she finds herself
Celebrating the anniversary of lies.
The lies have increase with the advancement of technology.

As the years go by, she has learned not to ask why
Why bother to prove to a liar that they are lying

As the years go by, she understands that a
Liar doesn't know how to be truthful
They invent lies.

As the years go by, she's learning to listen to the voice of her
Parents. Don't expect a person to give what they don't have.

As the years go by, she has come to the understanding that
A liar is like flies,
You don't have to be dead meat for them to spread their germs
On you. With the click of a mouse, they
Build for themselves a house
Of lies.

As the years go by, she is discovering that liars
Don't just lie because they want to,
They tell lies to hide deep, dark secrets of self-hate.
If they are not happy, no one should be happy.

Stay away from people who like to talk about
What they hear someone say about you,
Most times they are the ones saying it.

As the years go by, she is discovering who she is becoming.
Who is she, you may ask?
She is a visionary; she looks beyond the present,
She sees the future the way it can be.
If she has enough wisdom, she understands that anyone
Who dares to change the world to make it better,
Will suffer from the backlash of the haters of peace and unity.

As the years go by, man, how they fly, yet
It seems like time has stood still.
Nothing really changed, haters are still hating, lovers stop loving
They blame it on the haters.
They claim that they are tired of loving,
Why should they continue to love and not be loved in return?

As the years go by and our children start to ask
Why they have to be nice,
Don't tell them why.
Show them how
They, too, will discover that love is the pathway
To heaven, health, and wealth.

New Way, New Year

A new year, a new week, sweet!
We are living in a world of social media,
The likes of which the world has never before seen.

The Good Book tells us that in the last days,
Knowledge will increase, and faith in God will decrease.

The human race is racing to destruction
In their quest to be what they think they should be,
They are forgetting who they were meant to be.

Everyone is living in the fast lane.
Mothers are not at home anymore, they are working
Two jobs just to get ahead, leaving their children
In bed with video games to babysit them.

Everyone is working for the American dream,
A house with a picket fence is not the American dream anymore.
Drones and phones are what the children want,
Children are swept up in the whirlwind of greed,
The grass is always greener on the other side.

It is said that children speak the language of their mother,
What about those mothers who can't be bothered with
Taking time out to teach their children real values?

When did we get to the place where '*what we have*'
Became '*who we are*'?
Kindness comes from the heart; it is like a
Delicate rose. It must be cultivated.

Anybody can do a kind deed if they know
That they will get one million 'Likes',
The question is, will you do the right thing
Even when no one is watching?

Raising children is hard work.
No one ever gets it right, we all mess up,
It would help if we fess up, so others can learn from our mistakes.

Give your child a hug. Show them love, talk with them,
Listen to what they have to say.
Don't be talking to the whole world while ignoring your children.

DEAR FATHER

Dear Father in heaven, please help me to live,
I don't want to only exist, help me to resist the temptation from
Procrastination of experiencing peace and contentment,
Please help me to understand that I was not an accident at birth.

Remind me, precious Father, that even Your one
And only son had His share of troubles,
Yet, He never grumbled or complained about having
To put on a sinful nature to save mankind.

Please help me to show kindness to one and all,
Please help me to build a wall that will keep out lies and gossip.
Dear Father, You are my only hope.

DREAMER

All Joseph had was his dreams and his good looks,
Along with a coat of many colors.
In the corner of my wild imagination, I can't help but come to my
Own conclusion that his grieving, gray-haired father had someone
Cut up his dead wife's clothes to make the coat of many colors
For his son as a living memory of her.

I find myself wondering what would have happened to Joseph
If he had abandoned his dreams.
When his brothers put him in the pit, why didn't he become bitter?
No one would blame him, because we would agree with him
That he had a good reason to become bitter.

When your dreams are bigger than yourself, you
Tend to see life or a giant-size TV.
When you are a dreamer, you create enemies.

Some will try to stop you from achieving your dreams.
When you feel like giving up,
Fuel up
Find a way to pull yourself up!

WHO ARE YOU TO TELL ME

How dare you try to tell me what I am
When you don't know who I am

You have a big mouth, and a bank account I can hardly count;
Your ego is dripping into the oil of your overheated imagination.

Why start a fire that you will not be able to extinguish?
I'm not a speech writer, you are my distinguished guest.
People buy our name to share in our fame,
Then we turn around and play the blame game,
Have we no shame

How can you have law with no order?
Don't blame it on the boarder
When we walk around with hate on our shoulders.

You are like an eagle with the eye of a needle,
Sitting on a goldmine, surrounded by your minions
Telling me what I can and cannot do
When you have no clue as to what I'm going through.

RACE TO THE TAPE

I will run to the finish line with the spirit of Usain Bolt
While borrowing the voice of Michael Bolton
To sing my freedom song.

I am a woman, a strong woman. I am a daughter, a sister;
I am somebody's aunt, I'm a mother, and yes, I am black.

I refuse to look back, so don't you even try to hold me back,
My mind is made up, I have nowhere to go but up.

Marcus Garvey said, "Up, you mighty race, accomplish
What you will." I will not let anyone drag me down,
You will never torment me enough to drive me over the edge to start
Destroying my temple with drugs, alcohol, sex, and greed.

Why should I act like a clown, life is not a circus,
I will chant and dance to the chorus of life,
I, too, have seen the light
See you at the finish line.

DON'T TELL ME

Don't tell me what I used to be.
Tell me what I'm doing now,
Today I declare to the world
That I will not bow out of the race of life.

Don't tell me what I can or cannot do, you need to be quiet.
May I remind you that you are not the boss of me.

Don't tell me what you hear about me.
As long as you live,
You will never understand me.

You are on a quest to bring me down,
But I will not allow you to bring me down.

Don't tell me who to be or not to be
Let me be, so I can be.

MOTHER

Loving you from a distance, I don't know your
Favorite color or what food you like. It is hard to explain the
Love I feel for you. I know that you love me even though
I don't remember you telling me that you love me.

I really miss having you around for the birth of my
Children. It was hard for me to listen to other mothers
Talking about their daughters, seeing photos of them
Holding their grandbabies, and going on vacation.

A mother is like no other, no matter how hard you try,
You can never replace a mother's tender touch.
I miss having you tell me that everything is going to be okay.

Mother, you are not afraid of anyone! Your mother was
Not around to tell you that she loved you, or to comfort you,
Yet you found a way to take care of yourself.

When life slaps me in the face and people try to bring me down,
I close my eyes and think about you. In my mind I talk to you, I
Hear your voice telling me that I must fight for what I believe,
"Don't allow anyone to use you and abuse you."
Thank you for the gift of life.
Loving you until the end of time.

THIS IS IT

"This is it. It's do or die." This was what she told me herself as she lay on the white sheet in the hospital bed. In the ER, a nurse comes in, "...name and birth date"; something inside her head wants to scream, "Mrs. Nobody!"

Her eyes were blinded with tears; tears that smelled like failure. About three years ago, she commanded herself never to shed another tear; she was tired of crying.

The nurse came back into the room. "I'm going to give you an injection." She took her sweatshirt off, revealing veins that would make any addict skip for joy. She closed her eyes as the nurse pricked her with the needle. "You have nice veins," the nurse said to her.

And so it was that she was injected with pain medication. She could feel the warm sensation rushing through her veins. Within five minutes, she felt like she was slowly drifting off to another level; one that could become comfortable.

No pain, no stress. Just her and the pain medication whispering in her ear, "*I can be your friend if you let me. I can be just a pill bottle away. All you have to do when the nurse comes back, and asks what your pain level is on a scale from 1 to 10; just say 10.*"

"Who are you?" she asked the voice in her head. "*The question is, who are you; why are you here?*" "I'm Mrs. Nobody from far away, and I'm drowning in the swamp of hopelessness. Why bother to even try?" she lamented.

As she lay on the white sheet on the narrow bed in the ER, like a raging river, her tears came rolling down. There was nothing she could do to stop the feeling of neglect she was experiencing. She used to be able to hide these feelings away in the attic of her mind.

A feeling of hopelessness sweeps across her like a funnel cloud. By then, the pain medication was wearing off, and the pain was more than she could bear; or so it seems. The nurse came back into the room. "I'm going to give you some more pain medication." she said.

Just what the doctor ordered, she thought. She took a deep breath and closed her eyes, hoping to be carried away into the Twilight Zone.

"What's wrong with me?" she kept asking herself. A voice of reason, like distant thunder, echoed inside her head, "What would you do if you wake up dead? What will happen to your children?"

She opened her eyes to get away from the voice inside her head. She turned on the TV, but the volume was not working on the remote, so she gave up the idea of watching TV. Who needs TV when your life is a soap opera in the making?

TELL ME

Presidents come and presidents go.
The earth will remain.
You may kill the dreamer; you cannot kill the dream.

Tell me this, tell me that, tell me what I want to hear,
If the truth be told, most people refuse to accept the truth.

Tell me a lie; tell me everything is going well.
Tell me about the tintinnabulation of the bell,

Tell me you are here to break this shell.
Tell me what I want to hear, and you will be my friend.

SOME WILL

You have to know when to follow the old path,
You have to know when to create a new path,

Some will leave footprints
Some will leave impressions

Some will leave blank pages
Some will leave empty promises

Some will leave disease
Some will leave laughter
Some will leave timeless treasure

NEW AGE

In this day and age of technology, we are
Suffering from cyber mom syndrome

Mothers are important in the life of a child. How
Can we sit back and watch the children fall by the
Wayside without lending a helping hand.
Is it enough to go to the graveside of a teenager and shed
A few tears and sing a song that says 'gone too soon'.

Is it too late for mothers to stop what we are doing long enough
To understand the reason why our children are dying so young.
Don't you see what's happening? Our children are drinking
Alcohol before they can buy it for themselves.
Who lights up the first cigarette for a teenager
Who gives them their first blunt to smoke?

Listen to me, this is no joke. Mothers, are we so busy working
Overtime all the time to pay for cell phones, iPhones, Xbox, that
The children get to keep them entertained, so mothers
Can be left alone to do what they want to do.
Mother, I beg of you, stop, I am begging you, don't let another
Child go astray without doing all you can to stop 'em.

MOTHER, MOTHERS

Mother, there is a price to pay for being a godly mother.
It is extremely hard to come up with the down payment.

Mother, it takes guts to watch your life slipping away from you
In order to give your children a safe and happy home.

Everyone openly speaks of the joy of a newborn baby. Tell me
What happens when the baby no longer smells new and fresh.

Alone again to pick up the pieces,
Alone again to keep the lamp burning.
I must do what it takes to keep my children safe.

Every child needs to feel safe in the place they call home.
School was not meant to replace the home.
Teachers cannot teach our children what
We as mothers are supposed to teach them.

WHY AMERICA

Why not America
She welcomes us; this is a land of dreamers.
The pilgrims were the greatest dreamers, leaving
What they knew to venture into the unknown.
With hearts of steel and lots of elbow grease, they worked their
Fingers to the bone in the quest of achieving the American dream.

Why America
Why not America
This country has an unseen force pulling people from
Every walk of life. If you ask me, I would be the first to
Tell you that this is why this country is so blessed.

The good old Bible tells us that those who take care of the widows
And orphans have the blessing of God upon them. May God have
Mercy upon those who have convinced themselves
That they are now god of all, telling themselves
That they know what is best for America.

History will tell of what is to come. Kindness is a
Language everyone knows, and I'm sure we all know
That it is not what you say, it is what you do.
Sometimes it is not what you do, but how you do what you do
Is the world asking the question, why America, why?

PEACE

There is beauty all around us. I'm here to see and hear
Listen to the birds sing songs of praise.

The gentle breeze that caresses the leaves,
Leaving behind the fragrance of roses.

The cloudless sky looks down on creation.
She covers the world with her blanket of love.

Close your eyes, open your ears,
Do you hear the voices of creation?
Serenity,
Serenity,
Oh, what peace.

AMERICA

Dear God,
Please protect America, help us to understand
That she is the mother of the world.

Please, Father God, supply her breast with extra milk so
She will be able to feed the children from all over the
World who are latching on to her breast for comfort.

America is a chosen vessel, the God of all. He is watching over
You; be strong, be brave, be bold, your story will be told.

America, I'm begging you, please don't turn away the sick
And hungry children from your front door; pump your
Breast, put the milk of compassion in bottles of kindness.
Share it with the needy, stop listening to the greedy.

TO ALL

To all the mothers who gave up everything in order for
Their children to become something. No one hears your
Silent screams; you are crying so loud, yet no one hears.

To all the mothers who have been fired for calling off too many
Times and end up in the soup line; not because you want to.
To all the mothers who are minimum wage workers; do you
Cry yourself to sleep nights, wondering when your break
Will come? You work so hard, yet you are not able to make it
On what you earn. Do you sometimes ask yourself what you
Have done to be treated like you are the scum of the earth?

To all the mothers who work in restaurants, doesn't it
Sometimes make you cry when you see all that food going
Into the garbage, knowing quite well that when you get
Home, you have no food to feed your children?
To all the mothers who have no voice, I will become your voice. Mr.
Politician, be you Democrat or Republican, stop slapping us in our
Face with your insults. Do you know what it feels like to have three
Jobs and still not be able to take care of your children? Do you even
Want to help us educate our children? We are of the opinion that
The plan was and is to keep us poor so you can remain in power.
To all the mothers who are doing their best to give their children
A better life than what they have, keep hoping, keep believing,
Keep your dream alive. Remember to always give what you
Have, read to your children, hug them, teach them to pray,
Weave a basket of hope and fill it with love and respect.

Stop

Stop using the poor, we are sick and tired of your
Lies. How long will you continue to speak from both
Corners of your mouth, stop using the poor.

We, the poor, don't want to beg at your door. Just pay
Us a little more, we are not lazy, even though you think
We act crazy. We, too, have dreams and aspirations.
You gave us freedom, yet you are robbing us of wisdom. We,
The poor, want to educate our children. We work our fingers
To the bone with nothing to show for our hard work.

We, the poor, built your empire from the ground to the
Cloud, why must you continue to treat us like clowns.
We, the poor, are not afraid of working hard, we feel
Downtrodden. How are we to survive? You only want to
Pay us part time, yet expect us to be available full time.
Have you no conscience? Stop using the poor.

We, the poor, are sick and tired, yes, we are sick and tired.
Yet we can't go to the doctor; no health insurance. We are
Stripped of our dignity and self-worth. Are we not like
Autumn leaves falling from grace to disgrace while you and
Your children sit in your high towers looking down on us
As crushed dust, woe to us, we have no one to trust.

MOVE

The weapon of my mind is more powerful
Than a thousand machine
Guns. I will use it to free my mind from all this pain and suffering.
I refuse to give up.

With God's help, I am going to keep pressing on.
Please move out of my way, I will never obey you.
Your ultimate goal is to break me.
You will not rest until I have to crawl on my belly,
Broke and broken and bowing down to you.

I will not allow you to take away my peace.
You are looking for company to share your misery.
Your identity is painful, your lifestyle creates mayhem,
And you don't know how to be humble.

You are always tripping over your stupidity, then you turn
Around and have a pity party. You live in the fast lane. All
You want to do is run in the name of having fun.
You will not break me into who you want me to be.
I am strong and brave.
I refuse to let you send me to the grave. Move out of my way.

MY JEWELS

My children are my priceless jewels; I will keep and care
For them with all the tenderness my heart possesses.

My children are my jewels; I pledge to God and myself that
I will love them with all the love my heart possesses.
Writers get their words copyrighted to make
Sure no one can steal their words.

My children are my jewels; I don't know how to get
Copyrights for them, but I know how to care for
Them in order to keep my mommy rights.

I pledge to God and myself that I will keep drug
Addicts, drunks, drug dealers, and child molesters away from
My front door. For this reason, I don't have many friends,
Don't have much time to surf the web

My children are like a bunch of roses, looking good and smelling
Wonderful. They are not perfect, but God chose me to be their
Mother, and one day I will have to stand before Him
And give an account for them.
My children are my priceless jewels.

HE DON'T WANT YOU

He don't want you,
He only wants a piece of you,
That is the only reason why he keeps coming back.

If he could find a way to cut off the piece of you that
He wants; he'd cut it and put it in his pocket,
Like a piece of pork.
It sounds funny, but it is not a joke.

WHAT

What does the word 'what' mean to you?
What did you just say?
What did you think of that?
What are you going to do about that?
What are you thinking about?
What do you want from me?
What am I supposed to do with this?
What do you expect me to believe?
What were you thinking?
What will they think of next?
What a mess
What a waste
What a shame
What a calamity
What a stress
What confusion
What is your name?
What is your phone number?
What's up?

WISH

I wish someone would send a message to the governor
That even a fool seems wise when he shuts his mouth.

I wish someone would send a message to the governor
To let him know that he who tries too hard to prove
He is innocence appears guilty.

Mr. Governor, I'm a high school dropout,
My voice will not be heard by millions,
But if by mistake someone should listen,
Justice is not justice until all is justified.
He that has an ear to hear let him hear.
Justice is not justice until all is justified.

BULLIES

Bullies will rise, and bullies will fall,
As long as we live, this is how it is going to be.
Bullies are like vultures flying over the weak
And fearful, spreading a spirit of fear

They don't care about your feelings; they are like
Cannibals who see you as nothing but flesh,
They will suck out your brain and pour your blood down the drain

They get a high when you are feeling pain; they are like vicious
Lions walking around in human body with a hole for a heart,
Acting smart, wearing red expensive ties and eating cherry pies

You have many kinds of bullies—fat, skinny, short, tall, some
With big hands small hands, rich bullies and poor bullies,
Bullies of all races, bullies in the poorhouse, bullies on the
Playground, and bullies in the White House acting like
Horses holding on to their manes with their tail in the air

Don't allow anyone to bully you, Stand up for what you believe in
Don't allow anyone to scare you into silence
Speak up for yourself and those who have no voice
Bullies will rise, and bullies will fall.

PAIN

Sadness is a song we all sing, some people are too busy
Doing everything possible in the name of happiness,
While undressing themselves to the demons
Of addiction, this they do in order
To cut off the God-given ability to be able to feel pain and sadness

If you cut your finger, it bleeds; if you slam your
Finger into a door, you use the F-word
The D-word the GDI, or you stick your finger into your mouth
Some even go as far as to use the same hand
To punch the door in its face
Some kick the door, everyone gives out
Something when they feel pain

Sadness is a part of everyday living; if you don't feel the
Pain of sadness today, it may come tomorrow.
A word of advice: don't try to roll a dice to see when it will show up
Be kind to everyone, even when you are feeling pain
Sadness is a song we all must sing.

POWER

The power of having power, He controls the world
You are the sunshine that repels the darkness

Give me power or I will die
Without power I can't take a shower

Who controls the power grid, hope it is not
Some lunatic from some faraway land
Or an eight-hundred-pound person lying up in the bed of delusion

Can you rely on Alliant for ultimate power
I really don't know, all I know is when the power goes out
Our inner voice speaks to us,
This is what it is saying: "Don't burn out your candle
Please don't put the kerosene oil lamp away"

In the hour of power, tell your doctors,
Please don't burn your paper trail
What will you do if Alliant energy
forgets the code to the power grid?

MY OVERWEIGHT FRIENDS

To all my overweight friends, I am not trying to single you out
I just want to give you a shout-out
Fat or overweight means different things to different people

Instead of getting mad when people call you fat or overweight
Why don't you take a good look at yourself,
And if you love what you see
Pat yourself on the shoulder and say you are looking fine
Treat yourself to some new clothes and rock what you got

If you hate what you see, don't assume
That everyone is hating you too
Yes, I know that some people can be cruel, but I don't waste
My time listening to what people are saying about me,
I try to focus on what I am saying about myself

This is what I would like you to do, get a
Full-size mirror, undress yourself
Yes, look at yourself, and while you are looking,
Open up the window to your soul
Pretend that you are marrying yourself for better or for
Worse, in sickness and in health, till death do you part,
Okay, open your eyes

Can you please do me a favor? Take a shower, make
Sure you wash the hard-to-reach places
Put on some baby powder, yes, invest in yourself. I
Want you to remember that beauty is in the eyes of
The beholder love yourself from the inside out

Be your own food police. What do you have in your
Refrigerator? Pop and more pop? What's up with that? I
Am not judging you, I am just trying to help you
Get rid of the pop, get some water

Your body is your temple, your mind is the reservoir of your soul
Shower yourself with kind thoughts toward yourself
It is not what they say about you, it is how
You feel about yourself that counts
To all my overweight friends, don't allow anyone to put you down.

WHAT DOES IT MEAN
TO BE AN AMERICAN

What is your story, why don't you want to share it?
Before you were American, who and what were you?
Do you even know where you are from?
Do you have white skin, black skin, or brown skin?

I am from Jamaica, I have my own story
Some say that my story has no glory
Why would you want to tell the world that you
Went to school without shoes on your feet?
That's embarrassing

Why would you even want to tell the world that
You never had enough food to eat?
As a result of that, you could not go to school most times
That's stupid

Don't you know that people are going
to judge you, not to mention
They will look down on your children and make fun of them?
Maybe they will

Have you ever stopped long enough to think about
History and the rise and fall of civilization?
We are all storytellers,
God gave us different gifts; don't be mad at me
For trying to use the gift He gave me
If cavemen could leave their story on rocks in damp dark
Caves, why must we live like there is no life after?

Our children need to know where they come from
How will they know their history if we keep it as a mystery?
We have to help our children find themselves in a
World that is filled with hate and destruction

I don't have to be an American to know that yes, I
Can be the change that this world is waiting for
Don't allow anyone to keep you in mental chains
Chisel your way out of dark thinking, open
Your mouth with understanding
Welcome to America where freedom lives,
For how long, I really don't know.
History has a way of repeating itself, time
To open up the history books
Don't forget to write your story; everyone is a part of history.

AUTOSUGGESTION

Autosuggestion lives in the blue house; he keeps you engaged
Whether you are alive or in the grave

Autosuggestion has a daily procession
The streets are paved with self-aggrandizement
That echoes across the human brain

Autosuggestion controls the mind of the thoughtless
With chants of good, better, best—NICE
Autosuggestion will give them no rest
He is the best at being the worst

Autosuggestion is all about he, himself, and only him
He is in the business of singing from his own hymnal
While the birds are sleeping, autosuggestion is tweeting
Captivating the minds of the thoughtless

Hawaii is doing the volcano split; the earth is spitting up hot blood
She is making everyone run
While autosuggestion is all about conclusion
What a confusion, where is the collusion

I Want To Know

I am in chains, can't stand this pain
Feels like I am losing my brain
Watching my life go down the drain
I am sitting at the fountain of youth
Let me tell you the truth
It feels like someone just hit me in my mouth, just lost a tooth

I must pay a toll for crossing over the bridge of death
Now I am starting to fret, my brow is full of sweat
The SWAT team of death is trying to eat up my flesh

I don't want to die, and this is no lie
When I die, where will my spirit go? I really wanna know
I am in chains, can't stand this pain

In The Name

In the name of friendship, you destroy our relationship
Why do you continue to live your life on the ship of confusion?

In your quest to discover the undiscoverable,
You turn your back on reality
While embracing stupidity, attending pity parties

In the name of friendship, you sell your
Soul to the gatekeeper of madness
You have so many friends, yet you are so very lonely
In the name of friendship, you have lost your human dignity

My Dad

Dad, you are more than a father to me, you are my
Friend; you are never too busy to talk to me
You always say that your children mean more
To you than all the riches in the world

My dad doesn't have much money
He doesn't have a home of his own
My dad only has a heart of gold that he shares with all his children
And grandchildren

Dad, I would not trade you for all the riches in the whole world
Many fathers have given their children money, power, and fame
For some, all they receive in return is shame
Dad, you have given us time and attention
May the Father of all fathers grant you a long and happy life
Love you…world without end

I KNOW

I know that I may never win a Grammy
But as long as I am a good mammy
That will be all right with me

I know that I will never be famous like Oprah
But as long as I can cook a good supper for my children
That is all right with me

I know that I was not born with a silver spoon in my mouth
But as long as I can find my place in life and
Find a way to make a difference,
I will be all right

TOMORROW

You can't make people happy; happiness comes from within
What I have let me freely give

I will enter into His courts with thanksgiving
And into His courts with praise

As long as we live, there are always going to be problems
Practice the power or praise and preach the power of forgiveness

Enjoy life as much as you can; it is a gift that
Can be taken away without notice
Tomorrow I will be happy, tomorrow I will show kindness

Tomorrow, tomorrow, don't tell me about tomorrow.
Tomorrow is for liars and cheaters
Tomorrow is a way of skipping today's responsibilities

Tomorrow, tomorrow, the mourners are standing by
The gravediggers are busy digging your grave
Tomorrow, tomorrow, you will not be able
To hear them say 'dust to dust'
Tomorrow, tomorrow, what about today
Dear Heavenly Father, please help me today
To stop and give You thanks for
Today's blessings

Too Weak

Too weak to think
Too weak to hope
Too weak to believe
Too weak to carry this load all by myself

Millions of tears I have shed
Too weak to shed another tear
Too weak to explain how I am feeling
Too weak to quarrel and fight

COME WHAT MAY

Come what may, I know that I will make it.
It seems like nothing is going right, but I know that I will make it.

I may not have the answers to life's questions, but I am making it.
So many times I feel like I want to give up
And hide, but I am making it.

Sometimes I just want to roll over and die.
I get tired of the ups and downs
Here I am feeling all alone
Trying to find a way to cope with all these feelings of loneliness
Come what may, I have to make it.

TRYING TO RISE ABOVE REJECTION

Feeling like a fool, for too long I've been fooling
Myself thinking that you cared
Believing in you with all my heart

Tell me what you think of me, am I the biggest fool you've ever met
If your answer is yes, I can understand
I should have known that it would end this way.

Let me confess that I am overstressed, dispirited, and discouraged.
It is hard to think that you would walk out on
Your family to start another family.

I should have known that you would change; I know
That people change. I may one day change too. It is okay
For you to stop loving me, but how can you even sleep at
Night not knowing if your children have food to eat?

I will try to make a new start; it is going to be hard,
But for the sake of my children, I will find a way
Go ahead; cling to your newfound love. I don't have wings
Like a dove, I am not able to fly anywhere. I will bear the
Pain for the sake of my children. I will not fall apart.

TRYING TO KEEP IT TOGETHER

Thinking of me trying to keep it together
Leaning on me to keep me going, leaving the past behind me
Making a change to face tomorrow

They say that life is like a road with many different signs
Seek for knowledge, and you will find her
Here are the words you must learn to speak
People are special; it matters not where they are from
Favor and promise are very good friends;
Sorry is a word not many like to use
Many sit and wait on tomorrow, I beg of
You, my children, use today wisely
Without wisdom, tomorrow will slip right past you.

Look above the confusion of today; know what you want out of life
Take responsibility for your own development
Thinking of me trying to keep it together

TRYING TO FOCUS

I don't understand you, you are like a busy
Stranger pretending to be the handyman.
I may have said some terrible things to you, but I did not
Tell a lie, unlike you, who made it your duty to lie to me.

I am frustrated and tired of trying to keep
Up with your changing story.
I am not mad at you for finding a young and
Shiny lover; honestly, I am over you

I have no guilt, I gave you my best even if
It was not good enough for you
I gave you what I had, stop trying to make me feel guilty
For doing my best to take care of our children.

Stop playing the victim, why do you feel that you
Should tell our friends that I kicked you out for a new
lover, stop hiding under the cover of Christianity

I am facing my new reality; sometimes I don't know
Where our next meal is coming from. In order for me
Not to hate you, I find myself praying for you.

Do you even know how hard it is to make excuses
For you when the children ask for you?
Yet whenever you get a chance, you try to paint me as a bad
Mother who stops you from coming to see them. Just so you
Know, I will wait on time to avenge me; for now I have no life
I will live through the eyes of my children.

Why wait until I have to push you? I know that
You think that I have done you wrong
Have you ever stopped to understand why I
Find it impossible to believe in you?
People see you as the lamb, and I am the monster. If I were
The monster you make me out to be, your children would
Be visiting your grave. I will leave you to time and God
'Vengeance is mine, saith the Lord'
I don't need your blood on my hands;
I am done trying to understand you.

Trying to Make It

Looking around me, what do I see seeking
For the answer for life's questions
Do you have the answer to my questions? I am
Looking at today with hope for tomorrow

Lord, please give me the will to go on, please give me the
Will to know that I will make it, my life is worth more than
What I am getting, please help me to give love and respect
Help me to open the door to true happiness,
I will never be afraid to love again

Love yourself without holding back, believe in the process of time
Today, things may be bad; don't be too sad,
You are the maker of big dreams
This is the price you must pay for becoming a brave woman
Looking through the window of time, taking
The time to make the change

REFUSING TO GIVE UP

Working toward a goal in life,
Living for something that is bigger than myself
I am more than a rib bone; I am a woman with spine and backbone

The pressures of life sometimes weigh me down,
Sometimes I feel like giving up
But when I close my eyes at night, I see my children
Smiling at me, telling me that they love me
That is when I remind myself my reason for holding on

Fearing God and no one else, I hear Bob Marley
In my head saying no woman no cry
I have a brain, and I will use it to get ahead. Don't
You dare tell me that I can't because I will.
I can do all things through Christ, who gives me strength.

INDECISION

Got paid yesterday—rent to pay, water and light bill
Not to mention buying groceries, my money is
Finished before I even cash my paycheck
I have to move at the end of the month, don't want to move,
But I don't have a choice, this house has been sold.

Can't find a house in town, I may end up
Going to live in the country
I am not afraid of living in the country, rent is
Cheaper, air is clean, but it costs way more for
Transportation, I am already on a tight budget

Lord, please bless my children, I hate to move them just when
They are getting used to not having their dad around, Help me to
Teach them to love You; I know that without Your help, I will fail
Sometimes I am overburdened with the
Cares of caring for my children

Sometimes I feel like I would just give up life, but deep down in
My heart, I know that I have to keep holding on, Lord, moving
Brings back sad memories of feeling unwanted and not feeling that
My parents loved me enough to make sure that I was taken care of.
Lord, I need You more than ever, for the sake of
My children, please help me to stay focused.

I Am

I am who I am, and you can't change me without my permission
I am heading where I am going, I am going where I want to be.

I love myself; I can't love others if I hate myself
I am not ashamed of who I am

I am not afraid of failure, most times your greatest failure
Is your ladder to reach up to achieve your goals

I am learning how to make it on my own
While reaching out to the ones I love
And reminding everyone that I am not above faults

I am who I am, I am what I am, I am afraid of no one, only myself
My life is no longer on a shelf, I have broken out of my shell
I am tired of listening to the tintinnabulation in my head
I am me and only me, I am what I am, who are you?

WHY

Why should I spend my whole life complaining?
Why should you spend your whole life complaining?
Why should we spend our time complaining
About things we can't change?

Why should I spend my days dreaming about
Tomorrow, which is not yet mine
And allowing today to pass me by without
Embracing the promises of today?
Why should you be allowed to take your frustration out on me

Why should I want to take that which is not mine,
Why should you take that which is not yours
Why should you ask me to do things you know I can't do
Why should I be made to sit in the dark
When I am afraid of the darkness

Why continue to do the things you do when
It means hurting other people
Why should I not give thanks for the good things around me?
Why must we try to change others when we
Find it hard to change ourselves
Why can't we be positive and leave the negatives behind us?

TELL ME WHY

Why do people fall in love, why am I
Always thinking about true love
Why does it feel so good to be in love with you
Why am I so happy whenever you tell me how
Much you love me and want to be with me
For the rest of your life

Why do I get these feelings deep within me
Whenever I hear your sweet voice
Why am I lost in the sweetness of your love,
Why are you so in love with me

Why are we not spending more time together
If we are in love with each other
Why am I so afraid to show you how much I am in love with you
Why am I afraid to embrace the love you have
To give me in the stillness of the night

Why am I wishing you were here with me holding
Me tight till our hearts begin to beat as one
Every time I hear the phone ring, I hope and pray as I take up the
Receiver that I will hear your sweet voice, but in vain I waited
Why didn't you call to say that you would not be calling again

I Need

I need to be alone, need time for myself
Need to be able to stand up tall
Need a moment of peace
I need an outlet for my anger, need to
Keep my head above the water

I need your love and respect, need your understanding
Need to know that you will be there for
Me if ever I should need you
I need to stay above the waves of life, need a
Comfortable place to lay my head

I need to see the sun come shining through,
Need to be free to be who I am
Need to be able to sit and watch the waves of the sea
I need the peace that only God can give, I
Need to live a life that pleases Him

THE WORLD IS MAD

I am living in a mad world, a mad, mad
World. I don't feel safe anymore
I feel as if I am going out of my mind
Why are we so hungry for blood, for rich red blood
Tell me why don't I feel safe living in this world anymore

Why all the shooting and killing, why should someone
Walk into a home and kill a whole family, even the dogs
Why, why, can someone please tell me why are they
Doing this? Are they being paid to do it?
Why should our children be afraid to walk on the streets
Why all the madness, why are we so ruthless,
Why must we go on like this
Why, why?

LADY, LADY

Lady, lady, with your hair touching your waist
Where is your grace, I don't see it in your face

Lady, lady, yes, you with your hair touching your waist
At what point did he convince you of his undying love

Lady, lady, yes, you are you his number one or twenty-one
You are acting like a twenty-one-year-old who
Has been touched for the first time

Lady, lady, yes, you with your hair touching your
Waist, are you only a stand-by generator
Or are you just a common fool trying to act
Classy, wagging your tail like Lassie

Lady, lady, yes, you the new old boss lady without class
How long will you continue to drink from your glass of stupidity?
Do you think for a moment that you are the
Only one drinking from his glass?

Lady, lady, yes, you with your hair touching your waist
You are trying to tame one untamable dog
How can you be so blind, quit trying to be what you are not

Lady, lady, yes, you with your hair touching your waist
You must be really wasted and washed up to
Think that you will ever be able to peel
An old onion without crying hot bitter tears

Lady, lady, with your hair touching your waist
When are you going to realize that for you he don't care
Lady, lady, with your hair touching your waist
Where is your grace, I don't see it in your face

'RAISON' IN THE SNOW

She is just a 'raison' in the snow, but that
Will not stop her from shining
This 'raison' in the snow will let her love show
By doing what she knows is right

'Raison' in the snow,
It must be really hard to be a 'raison' in the snow
When you are from the island in the sun

She is a 'raison' in the snow, building snow
Castles instead of sandcastles
'Raison' in the snow, why did you trade your
Sun and fun, not to mention
Your rum and Easter bun in order to become a 'raison' in the snow

'Raison' in the snow, you bring sunshine and
Smiles by going the extra mile
'Raison' in the snow, 'raison' in the snow
How long will you continue to do what you are doing?
'Raison' in the snow, 'raison' in the snow
Don't you miss your island in the sun?

THIS IS MY LIFE

This is my life, I will not run away from it, and
Even if I could, I would choose to keep it
This is my life, I refuse to allow anything
Or anyone to break me into pieces
No, no, my friend, I will not let you throw your fears on me

This is my life, I don't need your permission to live it
I am my own woman, brave and strong;
This woman is not afraid of falling
My rise and fall are what give me strong backbones

This is my life, I have fears, I have weakness; believe me
When I tell you that I have tasted bitterness, the bitterness
In my life I have learned to use them like aloe vera
Even if no one gives me permission to live, I
Will survive a million stormy weathers

This is my life; I am shining and glowing even though I am hurting
My dear friend, if you are trying to break me, you
Are too late, I have already been broken
Some people were meant to be broken in order
To stop others from being broken

This is my life, I really don't need a
Stockbroker to manage my emotions
I don't have to create a commotion in order
To tell you that it is what it is

I have a gold mine, and it is not between my legs—it is in my head
I am not your porn star, so don't expect me to
Sleep with you in order to get a raise
I am not your braised pork

This is my life; I will never allow you to pull me apart
I am keeping my heart clean while reminding
Myself never to drink from your stream
This is my life, I will never let you or anyone kill my dream

LYING KNIGHT

You are a knight in lying armor
Using your tongue like a hammer
Talking from both corners of your mouth

You are a knight in lying armor
Telling lies just to get by
Your victims are low self-esteem fools
Who allow you to use them as your tools

You are a knight in lying armor
Waiting at the harbor like a barber ready to cut
the hair off the simpleminded fools
Looking for a friend to climb up the smoke stairs that lead nowhere
You are a knight in lying armor

WOUNDED GIRL

Good morning, little wounded girl
Did you remember to say your prayers
Before you went to bed last night
Whatever you do, please remember to put a smile on your face
Try not to wear your pain on your face.

Little wounded girl, you are almost sixty years old;
It is time for you to stop being afraid
It is time for you to face the giants and the bears from your past
That is the only way to put the past behind you.

Little wounded girl, in order to heal, you
Have to allow yourself to feel
Man-made medicine cannot cure a wounded soul
Your emotional closet is full; time for you to start pulling stuff out
In order to make room for happy emotions

Little wounded girl, don't let them keep you in a corner anymore
Swim through your ocean of tears, pull yourself up
You have to be strong, you have to be brave
Sometimes being strong means allowing your weakness to show
You have to let go of hurtful emotions
Even the mighty ocean has a way of spitting
Out the garbage it doesn't want
Little wounded girl, it is time to heal.

MONOLOGUE

I was judged by a judge who lacked judgment. He
Gave me no time to comment, leaving me to lament
The lack of commitment, seeking out justice
I was only looking for help with forcing him to help
Take care of his children. Was I looking for alimony? No,
Not at all. All I wanted was to answer the call of being
A good mother who was willing to put her life on hold
In order to give her children what no one gave her.

Your Honor, thanks to you, I have spent sleepless nights, shed
Millions of bitter tears, trying to change the unchangeable.
I never intended on becoming a rebel, yet I got rolled into
The grave, trying to grapple with being a single mother while
Trying hard not to open the door of childhood trauma of being
Molested and sworn into keeping a secret that should have
Been no secret if I had a mother to talk to about my pain.

Your Honor, when I came to you, I was only trying to change
My past by doing my best to take care of my children. I
Never wanted any of my children to feel unwanted. You
See, I made a promise to myself when I was a young girl
That when I became a mother, I would do everything in
My power to be the best mother to my children.

I fear for my children going through unnecessary pain and trauma
Like what I had forced upon me when I was a child. Your Honor,
You are not able to comprehend the feeling of shame and blame that
I have had to live with. My parents were not there to protect me.

Your Honor, I have no idea what under God's heaven possessed
You that you could even justify treating me like you did.
When I came before you, I was at a breaking point.
Lost my job, no money in the bank, husband was living with
Another woman, taking care of her and her child, landlord wanted
To sleep with me in lieu of rent. Maybe if I had entered his tent of
Deception, that would have solved my money problem, wouldn't it?

So, Your Honor, in my defense, I could have taken your advice.
Remember how you told me to send my children to the poorhouse?
At that time I never truly understood what a poorhouse was.
All I know is when you uttered those words out of your
Mouth, I felt like someone just shoved a sharp knife
Into my belly and twisted it from side to side.
All my childhood trauma came gushing out. I wanted to
Shout and scream, but I was afraid that you, Mr. Unjust
Judge, would have charged me with contempt.
I felt helpless; in just a little while, I would be
Homeless. Should I just give up the fight?

After crying and crying over and over again, I reminded myself
Of what I had been through as a child. I told myself that I would
Rather die than allow my children to be exposed to the evil that
Walks around in the form of incest and rape and child molesters.

Your Honor, in my defense, I refuse to roll over and play
Dead. I am going to use my head. I went and did a course
In hospitality and hotel training. By the time I got a job,
I had to make the hardest decision of my life; splitting up
My children with the hope of reuniting with them.

Your Honor, in closing, please allow me to present you with
Some cold, hard facts. A girl who had been molested would
Find it really hard to trust anyone unless they got treatment.
Trust is like a wall that takes time to build, so you see when
It is torn down, before you have a chance to build it, you
Are not able to tell anyone about your deep, dark pain
If you are lucky enough to fall in love, then get
Your wall of trust and respect shred to pieces
You may never again trust anyone.

If by any chance anyone gets the chance to read this monologue,
I have traveled halfway around the world holding on to
My dream of trying to be a positive role model to my
Children and helping them to become good citizens.
Don't ever exchange your morals for money or fame.

My childhood was taken from me. I will fight for my children's
Safety. I wish I were able to speak up before now. I would have
Spared myself a lot of lonely nights and a few less gray hairs.
Pain is like water in a dam; when it is full, it has to find an
Outlet. Some take drugs, alcohol, and even religion to hide
Their pain, so this is my way of opening the curtain that
Leads to my innermost pain. In speaking up, I may help my
Children and their children understand that no one is above
The law; even church leaders sometimes do bad things.

Finally, I am not sure if anyone cares about the children who
Get lost in the transition of painful emotions. I am a product of
Pain, and feeling ashamed of carrying around a shameful secret.
These days I find myself re-living childhood
Memories with all the #MeToo movement,
And the death of my firstborn, who was too afraid
To talk about her personal pain to anyone, so she
Went to her grave with a secret well kept.
I can't help but wonder if things would have turned out differently
If I would have been brave enough
To open up about my personal pain.

Your Honor, I am not able to change the past. Wish I could
Bring my daughter back from the grave, but I can't. All I
Know is what I know and how I feel. If you would have been able
To Treat me with respect and treat me like I was your daughter, you
Would have never uttered those words from your mouth.
If I wanted to send my children to the poorhouse,
I would not have come to you for help.
I am a product of pain and shame,
But I refuse to play the blame game. I will
Rise above the state of melancholy.
Mr. Unjust Judge, you couldn't break me.
You helped me to become stronger.
I now sing songs of praise to God. He will be the ultimate Judge.

What Do You Say

What do you say to a teenage boy who has lost his
Way and is finding it hard to pray to God?
His parents are the door that leads to God, and they have
Let him down, leaving him alone to fend for himself.
How can anyone blame him for acting out?

How do you reach a teenage boy who has lost
His joy; he is too old to play with toys
He is six foot two and feeling so much pain,
Pain that sticks to his heart like glue
How can anyone blame him if all he wants to
Do is stay home and sing the blues?

What do you say to a teenage boy who is trying real
Hard to be brave with his mother in the grave and
Daddy has a new family in the good old USA
What can you say to him about how he is feeling without
Hurting his feelings when none of his grandmothers
Are around to cook him some soul food? How can you
Call him a fool for not wanting to go to school?
What do you say to a teenage boy whose mother is dead, lying
Miles away in a grave with worms eating out her brain, while he is
Trying to real hard to control his raw emotions swimming in the
Ocean of rebellion, acting like a rebel because of fear, getting the
Feeling that no one cares about what he is going through? What
Can you even say to help this teenage boy who has lost his joy?

She Is

She is the villain
She is the one everyone loves to hate, and hate to love
She is the one they all wanna bake in their pie of delusion
As they come to their own conclusion while
They hallucinate at the gate of pity
And self-induced misery as they fry their brains trying
To kill the pain, watching their life go down the drain,
Blaming the law for them becoming outlaws
She is the one they all call the villain; the ultimate high

THEY

Who are they
Why is everyone talking about they
They who? Who they?

Please allow me to take the *T* off *they*
Hey, I am talking to us
Please stop pointing your fingers on *they* and *them*
Let's shift the focus on *us*

EPILOGUE

I am flying back home on a return trip from Jamaica after burying my first daughter. In spite of the sadness, I am still going to try and maintain my laughter and deep appreciation for all my children.

A daughter is a prized possession, but if the truth should be told, our children are not ours as God has only lent them to us for a time. With this thought, I have decided that I will live without holding back. I will turn my back on the cloud of sadness. I am embracing the love and laughter my sweet daughter left behind. She was an angel with a broken wing in human form.

She was not able to conform to the norm. She was like the sun; she lit up the darkness around her. It is so sad that most times we do not realize what we have until it is gone. The bond of a mother and daughter is unbreakable.

My daughter was not a rebel, yet she rebelled against the spirit of bondage. Her heart was pure, and her smile was contagious. She was not one to stay around and complain. She bore her internal pain in silence while spreading her wings toward the wind. When I think of her, I feel sad, yet I am happy that she is in a better place. Sometimes my eyes start to cry, then all of a sudden I am able to dry my tears. I see her pearly white teeth smiling at me. It makes me feel uniquely blessed to be the one who brought her into the world.

I would be lying if I did not tell you that at times I am not mad at God. Why did I have to lose my child to untimely death? Then I hear a voice asking me how do I know that her death was untimely when you find yourself at the roundabout of unexpected pain and suffering. It is up to you to decide if you are going to continue going round and round in the cycle of pain and sadness and self-pity, or will

you use your God-given wisdom to move on with the wind on your back and your head held high.

While I am stewing in angry thought, I admittedly reflect upon the realization that I may be missing other blessings. Am I forgetting to give thanks for my other two daughters and my three sons?

Dear God, please forgive me. Help me to live and love without holding back.